About the Author

Janice Jones was born in Nuneaton, Warwickshire, on 4th December 1947. After attending the local junior and high school, she gained a place to study physics at Oxford. She began work in the Personnel Department of a large electronics company, but gave it up for marriage and children (as was customary then). She had two children, but sadly the marriage did not survive, and she found herself pursuing a new career in teaching. She eventually remarried and finally moved to live in Spain.

Baby Boomer – A Post-War Chronicle

Janice Jones

Baby Boomer – A Post-War Chronicle

Olympia Publishers
London

www.olympiapublishers.com
OLYMPIA PAPERBACK EDITION

Copyright © Janice Jones 2025

The right of Janice Jones to be identified as author of this work has been asserted in accordance with sections 77 and 78 of the Copyright, Designs and Patents Act 1988.

All Rights Reserved

No reproduction, copy or transmission of this publication may be made without written permission.
No paragraph of this publication may be reproduced, copied or transmitted save with the written permission of the publisher, or in accordance with the provisions of the Copyright Act 1956 (as amended).

Any person who commits any unauthorised act in relation to this publication may be liable to criminal prosecution and civil claims for damage.

A CIP catalogue record for this title is available from the British Library.

ISBN: 978-1-83543-617-2

This book is a memoir. It reflects the author's present recollections of experiences over time. Some names and characteristics have been changed, some events have been compressed, and some dialogue has been recreated.

First Published in 2025

Olympia Publishers
Tallis House
2 Tallis Street
London
EC4Y 0AB
Printed in Great Britain

Dedication

To all those Baby Boomers who survived a childhood in which there was no TV, no mobile phones, no social media, no email, no *Snapchat*, no *WhatsApp*, no *Zoom*, no calculators, no computers, no PlayStation, no *Netflix*, no influencers, no bloggers, no apps, no factor 50 suntan cream, no digital cameras, no fitted bathrooms, no inside toilet, no school-run, no supermarkets, no duvets, no bottles of water, no UPFs (Ultra Processed Foods), no plastic bottles, no polystyrene food containers, no iPads and when a cookie was something you dunked in your tea and a tablet was something you took when you were ill.

And to the Alpha Generation – those born in the early 2010s; the first generation to be born in the twenty-first century and the third millennium and to a totally digital world – who might like an insight into what life was like for their grandparents and into the attitudes and events which shaped the world they now inhabit.

Acknowledgements

To my late husband, Gareth, without whose influence over thirty years of marriage, I might not have been inspired to write this book.

Introduction

My primary interest was always science, and I dropped history fairly early in my school career. However, retirement has given me the opportunity to pursue wider interests, and it occurred to me that members of the Baby Boomer generation – those born just after the Second World War – have lived through events of immense impact, both nationally and internationally, seismic shifts in attitude and dramatic changes in circumstances, opportunities and aspirations.

In Part 1, I attempt to weave my recollections of international and national events of importance into my own descriptions of circumstances throughout my life from working-class background to Oxford, working in industry, marriage, teaching and having children to chronicle the changing experience of a generation.

In Part two, I continue from two days after my mother died, when my husband chose to tell me he had been having an affair and wanted a divorce, through bringing up two boys, my working life, doing an OU degree and finally meeting Gareth.

In Part 3, I recount the romance every woman should have, and my life married to Gareth, the blending of our families, attempting to save a school in Wales, moving to London, buying our holiday house in Spain and ultimately moving to live in Spain; my 70th birthday present of a diagnosis of breast cancer, Gareth's son, Glyn's, death, and finally Gareth's death, cataloguing the immense changes in technology and events such as COVID, which have revolutionised how we all live and work.

Part 1

Chapter 1
Pre-School and Junior School

I was born on 4th December 1947, three weeks early, which was fortuitous because had I been born on Christmas Day, my mother intended to call me Noelle or Carol, and on the whole, I prefer Janice. My brother, John, had been born on March 18, 1946, but I was in my teens before I worked out that he must have been conceived on Armistice Day. Presumably, my parents decided they did not want to bring a child into the world during wartime and succeeded using such limited methods as were available at that time.

My father was a sheet metal worker, and during the war, though he kept volunteering, wanting to join the RAF, they kept telling him, 'You are more valuable building spitfires.' He was often sent down to The Bristol Aeroplane Company if they had a problem because Coventry sheet metal workers had a very high reputation. My mother had worked in the Courtaulds Textile factory and was employed packing parachutes. Growing up, I heard many war stories from them. Nuneaton is close to Coventry, which was famously bombed, and the term "to Coventrate" was coined. On the day after the raid, my mother and father went to Coventry and saw the devastation. About the only thing they could see standing was a huge sign for the performance at the cinema, which was fittingly *Gone with the wind*. Nuneaton itself was bombed because it was an important railway junction, though when the bombs started falling, everyone at first assumed that the target was Coventry.

On being told about the "terrible winter of '47", I thought, *Oh, I was born in the middle of that*, until it was pointed out to me that the winter of '47 meant January, February '47, not December '47.

My mother had a very hard time with it because my brother had failed to develop and was diagnosed with Coeliac disease, which was less common and more difficult to treat than it is today. Apparently, at one time, he was fed only bananas with a thick black meat extract over them. So, with an ailing two-year-old and a newborn infant, it was hard for her; however, we both thrived eventually.

Being so young, I was unaware of the so-called "Windrush Generation" people of Caribbean origin invited to come to Britain for jobs and a better life, contributing to the rebuilding after the war. However, later, in 1981, I was to understand why the then Prime Minister, Theresa May apologised to the people concerned.

We lived in a terraced house in a street in Nuneaton, a small town in Warwickshire. The terrace consisted of eight houses with an alleyway at each end round to the back, which cut the small back gardens into two, except for the two middle houses (of which ours was one,) where the alleyway just finished at a gate into the garden, leaving it uninterrupted. The front garden (if you can call it that) consisted solely of a tall hedge with a dirt area of about two square metres offering some privacy to the front windows from the street. There was no bathroom and an outside toilet. During our time there, my parents arranged for a bath to be fitted in the kitchen. The man who came to fit it must have been very irritated by this three-year-old pestering him as to why he was not putting in a hot tap – I didn't realise that just putting in a tap instead of blanking the hole would not produce hot water. I remember my brother and I having baths in about 3 inches of water, which had to be warmed up by adding kettles of hot water, but it was great fun as we could swish the water backwards and forwards.

I attended the local junior school, albeit about a mile or two walk away. I couldn't wait to go to school since most of my friends were my brother's age, and they had all started two years earlier. Being a sheet metal worker, my father was able to buy a very cheap old car and renovate it, while a friend did the mechanical bits, but we were never taken to school. The car was strictly for Dad's use, mainly for him to get to work. In those days, strange as it might seem, there was no driving test – you just got a car and drove! My mother walked us to school on my first day, but after that, as was customary in those days, my six-year-old brother and I walked on our own together. The school was called Fitton Street School even though the entrance was actually in Frank Street.

It is now called Chilvers Coton Community Infant School. A flight of stone steps went up to the left and right from the street level to the tarmac of the playground, which was at a higher level. The girl's side was to the left of the building, marred by the coal store (open to the elements and the children!) and by the toilets; rudimentary cubicles. The boy's side was to the right. The area in front of the building could be used by either gender. A low concrete wall separated the playground from the steps and the street below, but, of course, though it was low from the playground side, it was much higher from the street as I was to discover one day when I was sitting on the wall and a boy pushed me so that I fell backwards quite a distance to the street below.

To this day, I do not know how I got home. At least I had the next day off! To the rear of the school were two prefab classrooms (there were overcrowding problems even then!) and a grass area with what we called "the apparatus" – a metal affair of ladders, poles and bars which was our main play equipment. Surprisingly, despite all our random activities on the apparatus and its hard ground base, I don't remember anyone being injured. Beyond that was a large, raised grass area leading up to the canal, but we were only allowed there on special supervised occasions. The canal was separated only by a low wire fence, but I don't remember anyone disobeying orders and endangering themselves on the canal path.

For us girls, the PE kit consisted of skirts tucked into knickers and little black "daps", and we revelled in teaching ourselves to "toss-up" (do handstands) on the tarmac against the wall and doing "back bend kickovers" simply by standing and dropping backwards. I loved dancing around the maypole, weaving coloured patterns with the ribbons, though I must admit, I did get irritated by fellow dancers who messed it up. I enjoyed sports and was the fastest runner in my year, but when I went to the town sports, I was amazed how much faster the other girls were. For lessons, we sat in wooden desks with lifting lids, and joined in pairs, which had a metal frame. At first, we were allowed to write only with pencils until we could manage a pen and ink without difficulty. The ink wells were set in a hole in the top right-hand side of the desk. Being left-handed, I found it difficult to dip my pen in the well, and it was very messy, but at least conditions were better than they had been for my mother, who used to be hit on the hand with a ruler if ever she picked up the pen with her left hand. The punishment for misdemeanours was "the line". You spent the morning break standing on a line in the hall instead of playing outside.

1952 was the year of the London smog. We did not have a television, so any news I had of it was in the newspapers. I remember the pictures, but I'm not sure that I understood that in the course of five days, thousands of people died. I learned later that the effect was caused by pollution and high pressure and that the original estimate of 4,000 dead was later revised to nearer 12,000. 1952 was also the year King George VI died, meaning Elizabeth went on an official visit to Kenya as a princess and came back as a queen.

I remember the celebrations for the queen's coronation in 1953. My parents and their neighbours hung strings of coloured lights and Union Jacks from the bedroom windows from one side of the street to the other and pasted silver shields with the Union Jack onto the outside walls of the houses. At school, we were all presented with Coronation mugs, with images of the queen, crown and flags on them (I doubt if many survive today!) I was very interested to see a TV programme about the queen's coronation recently, because, at the time, we didn't have a TV to see it on. With the coronation of King Charles III, Baby Boomers are members of a small group to witness two coronations in one lifetime.

My brother and I belonged to the ABC Minors, a club for youngsters at the cinema at the end of our road, and we went there every Saturday morning for 6d. It had an organ which rose up out of the floor. One of our favourite film items was "Dan Dare". Apart from these Saturday morning visits, I can only remember going to the cinema once to see a film about the conquest of Everest by Sir Edmund Hilary and Tenzing Norgay.

The modern generation may think they invented recycling, but back then fish and chips came wrapped in yesterday's newspaper, and you bought bottles of pop in glass bottles for which you received 6d if you returned the bottle – a much better incentive than charging 15p for a plastic bag. Milk was delivered to the door by horse and cart, and you put tokens into the washed bottles on the doorstep for the next day's milk. It was some years before milk began to be delivered in small electric-powered vans. Coal was also delivered by the coalman on a cart pulled by a horse. Even the horse manure was scooped up by householders to fertilise the roses. Another horse-and-cart visitor was a man who collected old clothes and bric-a-brac and would negotiate a price. He would call out as he came around, but it was years before I deciphered that he was saying, "rags and bones".

"Make do and mend" – the mantra from WWII – was still prevalent. In the window of "Sketchley" dry cleaners, sat a woman mending nylon stockings on a machine that used to fascinate me. Whenever my mother took clothes to be cleaned, I would sit and watch the woman, trying to understand how the machine worked. Tights were virtually unheard of then – it was not until the mini-skirts of the sixties that they became more familiar than stockings. Many items of clothing needed to be dry-cleaned; only cotton, which was very expensive, could be hand-washed and then needed to be thoroughly ironed. There was a cobbler at the end of our street. Leather goods and shoes would last for years by being resoled. Men used to wear shirts with "loose collars" held on by collar studs so that when the collar wore out before the rest of the shirt, they would just buy another collar, not a whole shirt.

I had a friend, Valerie, who lived along the street. If I went to call on her on a Wednesday, I would be told "she's at Brownies", so I decided I would join too. We would be given 3d for our "subs" and 3d to spend in the sweet shop en route.

When I was eight years old, we moved to a semi-detached

house on Greenmoor Road, on the outskirts of Nuneaton. My father's boss had just bought a house in the "Whitestone" area of Nuneaton and had tried to persuade my father to buy one too, but at £2,000 my father felt it was too much of a financial risk. Many years later, when he had just bought his first ever new car for £1,750, I pointed out to him that he had just paid more for the purple Austin Allegro than he had paid for the house. The house had a front garden and a shared driveway to park a car. The back garden was relatively large and still contained an air-raid shelter, which my father, finally, with a great deal of effort, managed to knock down, but not before we had had much fun using it as a Wendy house and seeing who could jump from the roof and land on the lawn (avoiding the concrete path) unharmed.

My father recycled the concrete to form two rockeries and a seat between them. Although it was a much more modern house than the one in Victoria Street, we still did not have a washing machine or fridge. There was a pantry off the kitchen, with a "thrawl" – a tiled, brick slab which remained cold. There was heating only in the living room. My father became an expert in using "slack" – sweepings from the coal house – to "bank up" the fire so that it would burn slowly all night and last just until morning. This house was much closer to where my grandparents lived in a village quaintly named "Bermuda", though, since it was a mining village, it bore little resemblance to the other "Bermuda".

Sadly, my grandfather died when I was very small, but I remember him standing on a little bridge holding my hand to show me the "little truckies" going down the railway track into the open-cast mine below. My grandmother never remarried. My mother, brother and I used to visit her every Thursday evening to play dominoes and whist. Though she was deaf and had a large hearing aid with a battery pack that went into a pocket of her wraparound apron, she always seemed to be able to understand every word my mother said to her. At first, I did not understand how she could talk if she had never heard words, but apparently, she only went deaf later in life. I never found out why she went deaf. Much later, she had a television, but she called it the "trallyvision" because she had never heard the word, only lip-read it.

As children, our favourite activity in Bermuda was to go along the main (only) street to the crossing gates and over the railway line, to the canal side and the brickworks where we could find the little pieces of brick that had been punched out of the bricks during manufacture to form holes in them, which we could use for a game of "fives".

The house had a small sunken yard between the back gate and the door, with the outside toilet at the far end to the left. My grandmother bred chickens, and I hated it when the young chicks were born because they were kept in the sunken yard, and I had to run the gauntlet of their pecks to get to the back door. There was a scullery, the living room and the front room, though the only time I saw the front room used or went through the front door was for my grandfather's funeral. To my surprise, the room contained an aspidistra on a tall stand. I thought aspidistras only existed in songs and novels. The living room was dominated by a large table in the middle and a range on one wall. The range had a wood fire in the centre with compartments on each side for oven cooking – no temperature gauges. Above the fire was a series of S-hooks for hanging cooking pots.

I was told that one of my ancestors had been a forger and when the revenue-men came calling, they hid the printing plates up the chimney. If the fire was lit at the time, I can see how they might have escaped detection!

Years later, when I visited a museum of buildings, I was astounded to look through a half door and see an almost exact replica of my grandmother's house, even down to the handmade rag rug on the floor.

One of the stories I recall my grandmother telling me was of my grandfather, as a small boy, being sent to collect his father's wages from the mine owner. They were actually paid fortnightly in arrears, but it was possible to go to "borrow" the week's wages at the end of the first week. My grandfather duly said, 'I've come to collect my dad's wages,' and was roughly told to come back when he had learned some manners. Apparently, it was necessary to say something along the lines of… 'Please, sir, would you be kind enough to lend my father his wages until next week?'

My grandmother described how she left school at 11 and was offered the chance to be a teacher at 11d per week, or she could go into service at 9d per week, but that was "all found" i.e. board and lodging, so she was made to go into service.

A German lady rented the house next door to us on Greenmoor Road. She was obsessed with George Eliot, real name Mary Ann Evans, the famous female author, who was born in Nuneaton. As is often the case in situations like this, the lady, not a local, knew much more about the local celebrity than we did. We knew of the writer, of course, since there are several features named after her in Nuneaton, such as George Eliot Hospital, George Eliot Memorial Garden. It is said that many of the characters in her books are based on local people – including an ancestor of mine!

The next-door lady pestered my father to take her to lesser-known places, such as South Farm, where George Eliot was born and Griff House where the family lived at one time. I was told that she used the pen name because women writers found it difficult to get published at that time, but in fact, some women writers were published. It is more likely that she disliked the trivial subjects and storylines associated with women and wanted her novels to be associated with her more scholastic works. There is also the possibility that she wished to avoid the scandal of her private life by living with a married man.

There was no indoor swimming pool in Nuneaton then; there was an outdoor one, next door to the abattoir, which was unfortunate if the wind was in the wrong direction. It was unheated and we got very excited if the sign in the paybox said 72 (22C). You took a metal clothes holder and went into the wooden shack where the changing cubicles were. You were supposed to take your clothes holder back to the paybox, but that cost money, so we all just left them in the cubicles. We taught ourselves to swim by standing a pace from the side and lunging towards it, and gradually increasing the distance – it was sink or swim.

When I was ten, in the top but one class of the junior school, and just before the top class was due to sit the 11+ exam. I was told to go into the top class because I was going to sit the exam as well, and there was a little more I needed to learn, like fractions and decimals. I was a bit bemused at first, but when I was told I might be selected to go to the high school a year early, I was delighted because I couldn't wait to go. I waited impatiently, going to school every day hoping this would be the day the results came in, only to be thwarted, but finally, the day arrived, and the teachers let me go out of school at two p.m. to meet my mother as she came off her shift at work to tell her that I was going to the high school in September. I learned afterwards that my mother was a little apprehensive as to whether I would cope, having to leave all my friends, but, in fact, by the time they joined me the year after, I was completely integrated into my new year group.

I was rather young to be a soccer fan, but I remember the headlines of the Munich Air Disaster when a plane crashed, killing most of the Manchester United players, the so-called "Busby Babes", returning from a European Cup match.

Obviously, we did not have electronic toys like Nintendo and Xbox. We played with train sets, Meccano (an engineering kit with wheels, plates, rods, screws, nuts and bolts) and Bayko (a construction kit with interlocking wall pieces, rods and baseboards). We explored the quarry, made dens and hides, and climbed trees. Throughout the late '50s, the hula hoop became all the rage. Hula hoops had actually existed in Ancient Greece, but a modern marketing campaign turned it into the latest fad.

Chapter 2
Nuneaton High School for Girls

That summer we went to Guernsey on holiday, and I remember insisting on taking my new school blazer with me and wearing it proudly.

September finally came, and I settled into the new environment. The legal minimum age to leave school was fifteen, but at the high school, parents had to sign an agreement for their girl to stay on to sixteen to take the O-level exam. It was not actually legally binding, and I do remember a great fuss when one girl's parents decided she must leave at fifteen to work in their shop.

The school had a triangular patch of grass in front of the building known as "The holy ground" because previous headmistresses' dogs had been buried there. We were forbidden to walk across it, and even though it meant a much longer walk around the edge, I never knew of anyone who took a shortcut across the grass. Our current headmistress had two most beautiful fluffy white Samoyeds.

I enjoyed learning; it quickly became apparent that I had a talent for maths, and in fact, I never got less than ninety per cent in any end-of-term exam throughout my time at school.

I got involved in all the sports. Netball at first; though I was too short to be really good, I made up for it in energy. Cricket, tennis and athletics in the summer. I decided to become a wicketkeeper because I thought it would be less boring than being out on the boundary somewhere, and it appeared I did have the speed of reaction necessary for the position. I had discovered at junior school that I was not really a fast runner, but on introduction to hurdles, I was smitten and spent most lunchtimes out practising with a senior girl who was county champion. I think my prowess stemmed from being so small; other girls jumped up over the hurdles, but the only way I could get over them was to do it properly.

Imagine my disappointment when the town sports came round to be told that I could not compete, since the youngest category was eleven years old on September 1st and I was still ten. I won the school sports against girls two years older than me in a time that was faster than the eventual winner of the town sports. The next year, I did win both the school sports and the town sports and was 4th in the county. After that, I endured the change from yards to metres; a disaster for me which totally disrupted my stride pattern, and I never did quite as well again. I later turned to 800 metres, which was then the longest event for women. For hockey matches, we did not have a "squad" with lots of subs as teams do now. We just had the team and two reserves, who only came on if a player was injured. We really needed the reserve on one occasion when an opposition player's wild swing of the stick hit me across the nose.

The game went on with the reserve playing in my place, as I was taken to the cloakroom by the other reserve, blood pouring from my nose. I was lying on my back on the cold floor, which is exactly the wrong thing to do. It was nearly an hour before it stopped bleeding, and for the next fortnight, I did not dare to blow my nose. It was very uncomfortable. It was years later that I discovered that it had been broken. I had an accident with a ski pole, and the investigating doctor asked, 'When was your nose broken before?'

We also did some rudimentary gymnastics, which I loved and much later, in my teaching career, revisited by taking a coaching qualification. The next year, we were introduced to lacrosse, which became my passion. I was selected for the county junior team.

My family did not go out very much, but I do remember a few events during my time at the high school. Dad drove us to Birmingham to see the big film sensation. *Ben-Hur* in "Cinemascope" which had a wrap-around screen, which was supposed to make the on-screen action appear to come out at you. By the time we came out to go home, there was really thick fog, and it took us hours to get home. We also went to Birmingham Airport for a fun ride in a Dakota aeroplane, which cost 10/- for a half-hour ride. In my mind's eye, I can still see the airport, which at that time consisted of a single, low, white-painted building with a tower on top.

For the first three years, the curriculum was broad, and in the 3rd year, we even did a term of needlework, a term of cookery and a term of art. In the needlework lesson, we made an art apron and a cookery apron ready for the next two terms. I'm afraid the needlework was a disaster for me, being left-handed. I followed the instructions, but, of course, it came out backwards, and the teacher just yelled at me for being stupid until she finally saw me pick up the needle in my left hand – even then, she didn't apologise. It is rather surprising, after that experience, that I took to dressmaking and made many of my own clothes throughout my life. Art was much the same when it came to calligraphy, and the teacher saw I was left-handed and said, 'You can't do it. You'll just have to sit there.' Making me sit and do nothing is about the worst punishment someone can inflict! The first cookery lesson was, "How to lay a tea tray with cloth and cutlery!"

I remember being rather confused during this time because so many countries seemed to change their names. Now I know that this was the era of decolonisation, with countries which had formerly been colonies of countries like Britain, France, Spain and Portugal becoming independent.

At the end of the 3rd year, we had to select subjects for O-level. Subjects were grouped, and options were given. Since I wanted to do all three sciences, the only real choice for me was to drop history and choose geography or German.

Apparently, when I was much younger, an aunt had asked (as aunts are apt to do), 'And what are you going to do when you grow up?' I replied, 'I'm going to Cambridge to do maths.' I got that wrong; by then, I had decided I wanted to do physics at Oxford.

The so-called "Cold War" – a state of tension between the USSR and USA had existed since the end of the Second World War. There was no open conflict between the two superpowers, but in any local conflict, one side would usually be backed by the USA and the other by the USSR, in a series of "proxy wars". In 1961, the Berlin Wall, built by the GDR (German Democratic Republic) to separate West Berlin from East Germany, was erected. It had guard towers and a "death strip" of defences such as beds of nails and anti-vehicle trenches. The East German authorities referred to the wall as "the anti-fascist protection rampart" and considered its purpose to guard against Western influences seeking to pervert the will of the people in establishing a communist state. Its real purpose was to prevent its citizens from escaping to the West.

It was not pulled down until 1990, and during its existence

100,000, people attempted to escape, with some 5,000 succeeding. The death toll was estimated at around two hundred. The Cold War between the USSR and the USA was the dominant feature of global politics for a long time to come.

The Thalidomide scandal surfaced in 1961. The drug had been in use since 1953 as a tranquillizer and for sleep problems and anxiety. It was its use for morning sickness during pregnancy which caused the problems. It began to be noticed that many women who gave birth to babies with deformities had one thing in common: they had all taken thalidomide for morning sickness. It is estimated that some 15,000 children worldwide have had to grow up coping with a lack of limbs and other problems. It has been called the "greatest man-made medical disaster". Victims and their families faced a long fight for assistance and compensation, but at least a side effect was a change in attitude to drug safety, with greater control and testing regimes. Thalidomide is still used today being found to be beneficial for leprosy and some cancer treatments.

Of course, as young teenagers, around this time, we were beginning to be distracted by pop music. I didn't have any devices to play records on, so it was jukeboxes and radio. Elvis Presley was the big name, having been around since 1956, and most of our discussions debated the relative merits of Elvis versus Cliff Richard, but then the Beatles burst onto the scene in 1962 and "Beatlemania" arrived. I could never have dreamed of attending a live concert or even seeing them on TV since we didn't have a TV.

For French, we had an "assistante" – a young French lady who did conversation lessons with us. She introduced us to the French heartthrob, Richard Anthony and we learned the lyrics to *"Tous les garcons et les filles de mon age..."* most of which I can still remember to this day. Surprisingly, I heard the song again recently, during the coverage of the Olympics in Paris. Nuneaton was twinned with the town of Roanne, and we were each paired with a penfriend. Mine was a girl called Suzanne Montagnier, and even though neither of us was a linguist, our friendship endured, and we are still in contact today.

In 1962, the new Cathedral in Coventry was opened to replace the one destroyed by bombing during the war. Its central theme was reconciliation, with the idea that the new should grow out of the old. In the old area was a cross made from two charred pieces of wood from the old cathedral. Almost everything about it was unconventional. It was designed by Sir Basil Spence with a sculpture of St Michael on the outside by Sir Jacob Epstein. Perhaps the most controversial item was the tapestry behind the altar designed by Graham Sutherland, though the somewhat spindly spire, which was dropped in by helicopter, was also much debated.

I was lucky enough to attend two events at the cathedral. Before the cathedral was fully finished, the chapel of unity at the northwest corner was opened, and pupils from local schools who were studying German were invited to sing at a carol service in German. The small, hexagonal chapel is beautiful, with a huge cross suspended from the ceiling and, candlelit, it was very atmospheric. I still prefer the words of "Silent Night" in German.

Following on from the Brownies, I had been in the Girl Guides and had achieved the distinction of "Queen's Guide". During the week of the opening celebrations, there was a parade and service, to which all the Queen's Guides in the area were invited, attended by Princess Margaret.

A rather more serious distraction arrived in the shape of the Cuban Missile Crisis. Though we were aware of the "Cold War", at our age, the details were mainly lost on us, but somewhere down the line, we had gathered that the situation was very serious, involving Kruschev's Russian nuclear weapons situated on the island of Cuba (in the USA's backyard and under the communist rule of Fidel Castro.) and the USA President John Kennedy. We even, rather dramatically, asked each other what we would do if we were told we only had half an hour to live. It is now generally agreed that the incident was the closest approach there has been to nuclear war.

That winter was also a big problem with its severity. Often referred to as "The Big Freeze", snow lay on the ground for seven weeks continuously. My father forbade me from cycling to school because it was too dangerous to attempt the sharp, irregular ruts in the snow as it melted slightly and then refroze. Our PE teachers tried to come up with ideas for activities other than rather boring walks in a "crocodile" around the streets of Nuneaton. I am amazed that no one was injured during the team games they devised, taking place in the changing rooms complete with clothes racks with pegs and hooks protruding at eye level. One member faced the rest of the team, throwing a ball to the next in line, then racing to the back of the line while the first member took the ball and ran to take the place of the one who had just departed and continuing until every team member had taken part. We were very competitive and ran hard, so it was a disaster waiting to happen.

As I mentioned, my family did not go out very much, but once a year, Mum and Dad went to his work's Dinner Dance and as my brother and I got older we were allowed to go too. We felt very grown up. My father was a very good ballroom dancer, and it was easy to dance with him. The event was often held at a rather grand venue known as the Hotel Loefric in Coventry. The hotel is named after Lord Leofric, the subject of the famous legend of Lady Godiva from the eleventh century. The Lady was famous for her beauty, goodness and piety and was loved by all her husband's subjects. Having sympathy for the condition of the vassals, she petitioned her husband to lower the taxes. He said he would, but only if she would ride naked on her white horse through the streets of Coventry with only her long blonde hair to protect her modesty. When she carried out the task, all the people of Coventry stayed indoors with the windows barred, except for one man, a tailor forever after known as "Peeping Tom".

As the O-level course continued, it became obvious that despite best efforts, science teaching at the school left a lot to be desired. We missed a whole year of physics because they could not get a teacher, and the chemistry teacher had been brought out of retirement. He scarcely knew which day of the week it was. Girls used to block the sinks, turn on the taps, and run to the downstairs cloakroom to see the water dripping through the ceiling. In the end, we had to take physics-with-chemistry because we had not finished the syllabus, so I took that along with biology, maths, Latin, French, German, English literature and English language. The top set took maths early, at the end of November, so I was still fourteen when I took the exam. One tedious aspect for most of us was having to use logs for calculations – no calculators in those days. Sometime later, my older cousin introduced me to the "slide rule" a seemingly magical device to do calculations. It was rather complicated to apply, but once you mastered it, it was better than doing logs.

When we were sitting our mock O-levels, the headmistress came into the classroom and said, 'I want you all to be very calm and walk to the tennis courts. There is something strange in the chemistry lab.' A small voice at the back said, 'We know – it's

Mr Higgins.' We were seated in alphabetical order and my surname was "White", so guess whose voice it was! While we were on the tennis courts, several fire engines came racing down the hill. It turned out that Mr Higgins had disposed of some sodium down the sink. Sodium is highly inflammable. It is kept in small quantities in a jar under oil and ignites or explodes in contact with air and/or water.

In the Easter holiday of 1963, we went on a three-week exchange visit to our French penfriends. I enjoyed staying with Suzanne and her parents, but I was a little homesick towards the end, having never been away from my parents for so long or having been abroad other than the holiday to Guernsey. Her father was a butcher, and their flat was above the shop. Her mother was a cordon bleu cook, and I was treated to all the French delicacies. I was taken on a visit to one of the farms which supplied the shop, and the farmer was wearing "sabot" – the traditional wooden clog-type shoes, and the ploughs were horse-drawn. I was astounded to realise, one morning when I woke up, that I had had a dream in French!

When our penfriends returned the exchange for the last week of term after we had finished our exams, my friend Jill and I decided we needed to give them more of an experience than had been planned by the twinning organisers, so we arranged a visit to the Cadbury chocolate factory at Bournville. The tins, containing a selection of chocolates, which were given as mementos of the visit, were from then on the go-to for school pencil boxes. When school finished, my parents took us and Suzanne for a week's holiday in Hastings on the south coast. It was at the time that the scandal of the Profumo affair broke, and it dominated the newspapers. Married government minister John Profumo had an affair with a call girl named Christine Keeler.

That was bad enough, but even more concerning to officials was that she had also been in a relationship with Yevgeny Ivanov, a Russian naval attache under surveillance by MI5 as a spy, and John Profumo was the Minister for War! Many friends commented that I bore a resemblance to Christine Keeler; I was not sure whether to take it as a compliment! Many years later, in 1989, when the film *Scandal* came out, I could see their point.

The 1960s saw a revolution in attitudes towards sex. The introduction of the contraceptive pill gave women new control over their fertility, though it is possible to argue that it took responsibility away from the men. Until then, a common attitude on the part of men was that there are two types of women: those you sleep with and those you marry. It was quite a common view to see men as "wanting only one thing" and women as fending them off. There was still a stigma to being "illegitimate" – born out of wedlock – and if a young girl became pregnant, her father might well insist that the boy marry his daughter; a so-called "shotgun wedding". I now understood why I had sensed some hostility between my Aunt Maud and my grandmother and why her wedding photo, even though it was black-in-white, revealed that she was not wearing a white dress. My Uncle George, seemed a very nice man. I learned that they got married, but sadly lost the baby.

At that time, homosexuality was still illegal. Alan Turing, a brilliant man, the hero of the cracking of codes with the Enigma machine during World War II and the originator of modern computer technology, had been prosecuted in 1952 and was offered a chemical castration as an alternative to prison. His career was ruined, and he died in 1954. It was not until 1967 that "The Sexual Offences Act" decriminalised the sex act, in private, between consenting males over twenty-one. The age limit was not lowered to eighteen until 1994 and finally to sixteen. Even after it had been decriminalised, there was still some residual disapproval of homosexuality, and many gay men did not "come out" for fear of rejection by their families and of discrimination. Prejudice resurfaced around 1980 with the outbreak of HIV leading to AIDS, which was at first seen as a gay disease and, indeed, was called "the gay plague" for many years.

Chapter 3
Sixth Form

My friend Lesley and I were jointly designated "School Games Secretaries". Our responsibility was to arrange the following year's programme of fixtures with local schools for each of the sports. In those pre-Internet days, it involved sending out postcards offering a date for a fixture, pencilling it in and waiting for a response before confirming the date. It would have been a very daunting task indeed, if it were not for the fact that many of the fixtures were agreed to the same date year after year, and all we games secretaries responded quickly, knowing how much difficulty it caused if a response was slow.

We had lessons called "General Studies" aimed at the exam taken along with A-levels, even though it only had the accreditation of O-level, but they also had the aim of making us aware of current issues and important historical figures. I remember reading about William Wilberforce, who was instrumental in abolishing slavery, and Grace Darling, the daughter of a lighthouse keeper, who participated in the rescue of shipwreck survivors. One of the main topics was the American Civil Rights Movement. Segregation had been illegal since 1954, but further legislation giving more rights was not until 1964 with the Civil Rights Act and 1965 with the Voting Act. Martin Luther King, one of the most prominent activists, was later assassinated in 1968.

For A-level, I opted for pure math, applied math, physics and chemistry; it was very unusual to take 4 A-levels in those days. Obviously, it was not an ideal start to my A-level studies since we had not finished the O-level syllabus, and to add to the difficulties, again, they could not get a physics teacher. I think the problem was that in those days, most science teachers were men, and men wanted the best jobs in boys' schools, not in all-girl schools. We ended up having to go to the local college of further education, about a twenty-minute walk away, so, even though our lessons were timed so that some of the walking could be done in morning break, lunch break or after school, we still lost some teaching time. The first thing the teacher said to us was, 'I hate teaching girls; girls will never understand electricity. Anyway, you only want another A-level to go with your biology, so I'm not going to teach you any electricity.' I was not impressed.

We did have a chemistry teacher, but he didn't always turn up for lessons or was late, and on one occasion the girls elected me to look for him (I often got volunteered for such tasks!). I found him in the prep room, cooking hot dogs over a Bunsen burner with the L6th girls. This was three weeks before our exam, and we were nowhere near finishing the syllabus. I was rather angry and asked him if he was going to deign to give us a lesson; if not, could he give me a copy of the syllabus so that I could teach the class. He pushed a copy of the huge textbook "Vogel", which goes up to university level, across the table to me and said, 'Here, use that.' I snapped and threw the book back at him (I missed). Obviously, I was distraught and thought that a moment of anger had just ruined my chances of any university place, let alone Oxford. I rushed down to the headmistress's office in tears and knocked on the door.

She said, 'Janice, whatever is the matter? Sit down outside

and calm yourself, then tell me all about it.' She was wonderful. Obviously, it was a serious offence, throwing a book at a teacher, but the first thing she said was, 'I want you to know that this will in no way affect your university applications.' She proceeded to say that she was sure I was mature enough to understand that for the sake of school discipline, she must be seen to punish me – it couldn't be seen that a 6th former, a prefect, had thrown a book at a teacher and got away with it – but that, in fact, she had sympathy with my actions. The teacher was later sacked for having an affair with one of the 5th formers.

My brother was doing chemistry at Liverpool University, and when he came home, he said, 'Hey, Babs, I'll test you to help your revision.' I did not have a clue what he was asking and discovered that we had done less than half the syllabus, and even what we had covered was of limited use because lots of questions involved comparing and contrasting the characteristics of organic with inorganic compounds, and we knew nothing about organic compounds. I agonised over whether to tell the other girls but realised it would panic them to the extent that it would destroy their chances, so I decided not to say anything – they must have known to some extent anyway. I set about teaching myself as much as I could in the little time remaining.

Not surprisingly, my A-level grades were not great (apart from maths, which was OK), but at least I passed; no one else passed chemistry or physics. When I told my teachers that I intended to stay on into the 3rd year 6th to take the Oxford entrance in November (that was the only way to do it then) one laughed, and another said, 'No chance. It's very difficult to get in, you know.'

Chapter 4
Oxford Entrance Exams

For university choices, we had to select 6 in order of preference. I was advised not to put both Oxford and Cambridge, as that would make the next university $3^{rd,}$ and some universities consider only 1st or 2nd choice. So, I had Oxford, Westminster College London, Manchester, Reading, Hull and Exeter. I later learned that Exeter is 1st choice only, so they rejected me. the other four each offered me a place.

I sat the entrance exams on my own in the sitting room of the headmistress's house. I looked at the paper and thought, *I have not been taught how to do a single one of these questions, but I'm stuck here for three hours, so I might as well try.* I distinctly remember one question which began by asking for a definition of blackbody radiation and then proceeded to give a calculation asking for the answer to be given in W/m squared. I had never heard of blackbody radiation, but if the answer was to be in W/m squared then it must be to do with the energy per sec in an area of 1 m squared, so for the definition I threw in a requirement that the area must be at right angles to the direction of the radiation (since most definitions have conditions like that) and came up with the definition that: "Blackbody radiation is the energy emitted by a black body per square m per sec through a plane at right angles to the radiation", which is correct. Now that I knew what blackbody radiation was, I got the calculation right too.

Sometime later, I was delighted to be called for an interview. Up until then, I had been prepared to be rejected, but as soon as I got to Oxford, I knew that was where I wanted to study and would be very disappointed if I did not get in. At St Hilda's College, then an all-girls college, I met three other interviewees. They all had much better A-level grades than me, but in discussion, it appeared that I had more success on the entrance papers than they did. I had no help at all with preparing for the interview questions, but I remember most of them clearly. One I found rather daunting was a book that we had been told to read before the interview. The tutor asked what I thought of the book. Well, what do you say? If you just say, 'Oh, I think it is great.' You sound pathetic, but it sounds very pretentious for a mere seventeen-year-old to be critical of a textbook, so I said I thought that it was generally clear and easy to understand, but that it made heavy weather of what is essentially a simple concept: "virtual work". She said, 'Oh, so you think virtual work is a simple concept, do you? Explain it to me,' so I explained what I thought the book was trying to teach, and a smile spread across her face.

In another interview, the previous candidate came out crying, which did not auger well; however, the tutor led me through a complicated calculation to do with electric circuits which I just about coped with, then she said, "How would you find out what happens if you made a small change in the resistance R?"

I said, 'Differentiate, of course.' (from the time I had been introduced to calculus, I had though it beautiful, so I loved differentiation); however, I did admit that the equation was so complicated that I would not be able to actually carry out the differentiation. She said, 'Thank goodness, a physics candidate who does not leave her maths concepts at the door. I wouldn't expect you to be able to do the differentiation; it's university level.'

As I mentioned, I had no preparation for the interviews, and I knew that my grades were not great, but I did at least have great enthusiasm for the subject. I had decided to subscribe to *The New Scientist* magazine in order to keep up-to-date with scientific developments, and that turned out to be extremely beneficial because one of the tutors asked if I knew anything about the significance of the omega minus particle to the SU3 Theory of Unitary Symmetry – I had just read about it in the magazine!

By this time, I was considerably encouraged, though by no means confident. The wait for the telegram was excruciating, and on the day the telegram might arrive, I was due to go to London for an interview at Westminster. My mother kept saying, 'I know it will come; don't go, it will be a waste of time, wait a little longer.' At last, when I dared wait no longer, I opened the door to leave. The telegram man had his hand in the air to knock on the door. I literally threw my arms round the astonished man, to which my mother said, 'Forgive her, that telegram says she has a place at Oxford.'

Three of us from our school were offered places at Oxford: Janet to read law and Jane to read history. That doubled the number of girls from the school ever to go to Oxford; to celebrate, the whole school was given a day off, but, to our disgust, not until after we had left.

Chapter 5
Post-School, Pre-Oxford

One evening, just before Christmas 1965, I was sitting in the living room at home when there was a knock at the front door. We were all surprised; friends and family used the back door. The man on the doorstep announced himself as the headmaster of Swinnerton, a local secondary school, and his mission was to ask if I would teach games at his school for the next two terms; apparently, they were desperate and my games teacher had recommended me, knowing that I was free until I was due to go up to Oxford in September. I was astounded; I was eighteen, totally unqualified, and with no experience whatsoever, except helping other players as captain of teams at school; however, he persuaded me that they would give me lots of support and that if I said no then the games at the school would be totally disrupted. Finally, with many reservations, I agreed.

In January, my teaching career began! The school secretary even had to explain to me how to open a bank account so that they could pay me and how to get a National Insurance number and register for tax. I was paid 2/3 of the qualified teacher rate, which at that time was £15 per week, so I got £10 per week. The head of PE was just grateful for me to be there, since without it he would have had to teach boys and girls together, which would have disrupted his whole activities. In those days, girls did not play soccer or rugby. He was a lovely Welshman, whom I assumed had once been a good sportsman but had had to give up since he walked with a slight limp.

I was eighteen but looked younger, but apparently, the pupils believed that you had to be twenty-five to be a teacher, so my naivety was not exposed. I felt very grown-up using my personal changing room, with the girls having to knock respectfully if they wanted anything. The first lesson I took was in the gym, and I drew heavily on the way we had operated in my lessons at school. I divided the pupils into groups and instituted procedures for getting out the equipment and putting it away at the end of the lesson. I insisted that they stopped and sat down at my whistle. I actually enjoyed it, and the head of PE discreetly walked past several times to see how things were going. From that point on, he relaxed, and we enjoyed a good working relationship.

The most enjoyable times for me were when we went swimming on Friday mornings. A new municipal indoor swimming pool had been opened the previous year, just across the field from the school. He and I stayed there the whole morning while groups were brought over in relays by their class teachers; there was a little free time in between groups, in which I felt very grand enjoying a cup of coffee with him in the café!

A very satisfying time was when I was asked if I would mind teaching a pupil for maths O-level; the pupils were not usually academic enough to take O-level, but the staff thought that this pupil might succeed if she had individual teaching. I was pleased to do it and even more delighted when she passed.

That summer I was camping with the Guides when the World Cup soccer was on; England in the final against Germany (I'm talking about the men's team – there was no women's professional soccer then). We all sat around a radio listening with bated breath when it was 2-2 at fulltime. We got very excited when Geoff Hurst scored his two goals in extra time to complete his hat-trick and win the match, to the accompaniment of Kenneth Wolstenholme's famous quote "They think it's all over – it is now."

Chapter 6
Oxford 1st Year

I might have been overwhelmed on arrival at Oxford, but the staff at St Hilda's College were so welcoming and helpful that I immediately felt at ease. They made sure you knew where to go, what to sign on for, who to go and see, what tutorials were arranged and when there were lectures and lab work sessions. All first-year students had rooms in college. My room was in the old building, known as Hall. It was not grand, but adequate. No males were allowed in the rooms after nine p.m., and we had to be in by ten thirty p.m., when the gates were locked. There were about 110 males and ten females studying physics in our year! There were four of us girls in St Hilda's. Oxford had a tutorial system of study; you had a nominated tutor for each topic, who guided your study with weekly sessions and set work, but it was up to you how best to acquire the necessary knowledge and understanding. Lectures were not compulsory; you decided whether or not you found them a useful way of learning. In those days, the main other option was textbooks – no internet! In a subject like physics, there is also a lot of experimentation in the labs. I went to the first couple of lectures on each topic and then decided whether to continue.

The "Freshers' Fayre" took place during the first week, where clubs and societies took stalls to explain what they had to offer. I signed up for trials for Lacosse, deciding there would not be time to play hockey as well, and joined the Scout and Guide club, which held weekly "Nosh and natters" sessions for members to chat and get to know each other and country dancing sessions. They also held a once-a-year campout.

I became a member of the Oxford Union – the world-famous debating society. There was a very pleasant bar and restaurant below the debating chamber, where most students used to take their visiting parents. One day, I decided to treat myself to a cup of coffee there. I was really rather overawed by the historic surroundings and so attempted to adopt a relaxed and confident demeanour. The coffee was beautifully served on a tray, with a paper doyly, biscuits and a small jug of cream beside the cup. I raised my hand to brush back a lock of hair which had fallen over my face, completely oblivious to the fact that I had just picked up the jug of cream in that hand. The result was a very undignified trail of cream slowly descending over my hair.

In early conversations, when I said I was from Nuneaton, the response was usually one of two: 'Oh, I've been through there on the train.' (Remember, the wartime bombing of the railway junctions.) Or 'Oh, yes, the monkey.' This was a reference to a political incident. Nuneaton was a long-time Labour stronghold, and a few years earlier, when the party had wanted a safe seat for their candidate Frank Cousins, they shunted the long-serving member for Nuneaton into the House of Lords as "Lord Bowles of Nuneaton". A newspaper's comment was "If a monkey was put up in Nuneaton with a label around its neck saying 'Labour', it would win."

Although my concentration was on adjusting to my life in Oxford and studying, I was not oblivious to outside events and was as stunned and dismayed as anyone else by the Aberfan Disaster, when a coal tip above the village of Aberfan, near Merthyr Tydfil in Wales, collapsed and slid down the mountain side, engulfing the Pontlas Junior School and killing 116 children and twenty eight adults.

We were told that the first term would be mainly revision and consolidation, but of course, for me, it was not! I knew little of it; the problem was I did not know what it was I did not know. I vividly remember trying to solve a set problem and being convinced I was stupid. Eventually, I went to Fiona and confessed my difficulty. She said, 'No, that's OK; you have started off right, now you just need to apply Stokes' Law.' I had no idea what Stokes' Law was. For a while, I was convinced there was another girl somewhere with the name Janice White, who should have got the telegram instead of me. At the end of the first term, I did vaguely consider not going back, but it was a good job I did not because when we went back for the second term and the work was new to everyone, I found that I could do just as well as the other three girls.

For tutorials, we were arranged in pairs and for the astrophysics module, Fiona and I went one week, with Maggie and Sue the next. The tutor looked ancient, and I worried that she would be teaching us what she had learned in her day, but my fears were groundless. One week, I asked if she could recommend a textbook so that I could do some follow-up work on what she had just taught us. She said, 'Oh, it won't get into the textbooks for a few years; we've only just discovered it.'

There was a series of lectures for the atomic and nuclear physics optional paper, which I wanted to take but, unfortunately, we had not yet done the work for the atomic and nuclear basic paper, so I struggled to follow it. One day as I left the lecture theatre, Professor Perkins asked me what I thought of the lectures, so I explained to him. From then on, whenever he made a point, he would look round the hall and finally rest on me; if I nodded, he would carry on, if not he would explain it again.

In the particle physics module, I was astonished to discover that our tutor had actually been on the team which had discovered the omega minus particle, the crucial prediction of SU3 Theory of Unitary Symmetry, thus validating the theory. (Remember the reference to the theory in the interview questions?).

I was accepted into the university lacrosse team and thoroughly enjoyed playing. In those days, the men's and women's games were totally separate, and the facilities for the women's team were woeful compared to the men's team. There was no changing room, and we had to change in college and cycle to the pitch. We did not actually have a team kit until I made a set of pleated skirts. One day, when I was cycling over Magdalen Bridge in kit, with my stick and boots on the handlebars, an American leapt into the middle of the road with a camera and said, 'Say, are you a real live Oxford Blue? I must get a shot. The folks back home will love that.' It is very different today, with men's and women's clubs combined and seven teams. Even the sticks are different.

Each year, WIVAB (Women's Intervarsity Athletic Board), the organising body for British universities women's games activities, organised inter-university tournaments and selection events for teams for WIVAB South, WIVAB North and British universities. I remember one in Harrogate when it snowed nonstop and was bitterly cold. Overnight, the churned-up snow froze, so the pitch was covered in sharp-pointed ridges. One girl fell and slid along the icy surface. When she stood up, there was blood pouring from thigh to knee. It was very extensive, but fortunately, superficial, grazing but very sore. In another one in Cheltenham, it rained nonstop and the pitch just became a muddy mess – I doubt if Cheltenham Ladies College pitches were playable for a couple of years. Two of us were racing to scoop up the ball and realised we were just sliding in the mud; there was no way we could stop. Her stick hit me on the right eyebrow, but the team said, 'You can't go off, you can't go off, we need you. It is too critical.' Because I couldn't see properly, I misjudged a pass, and the ball caught the edge of my stick and flew up into my left eye, so I went home with a black eye and a cut across my eyebrow – when I had just about convinced acquaintances that Lacrosse was not dangerous!

On Tuesday lunchtimes, I used to practise with the university swimming team – not that I was good enough to be in the team; it was just that the pool was available, but I had a tutorial across the other side of Oxford immediately afterwards, so I rode very quickly on my bicycle (most students rode bikes). To my surprise, a police car stopped me, and the policeman said, 'Do you realise you were speeding? 31 mph in a 30 limit.'

I apologised and added, 'Well, it was downhill with a following wind!' Fortunately, he decided not to arrest me.

In the summer term (called Trinity term in Oxford), I played cricket for the university women's side. We did not have our own pitch, so we played on the men's college pitches when they were not being used, which was very tricky to arrange. Women's cricket was fairly rare in those days, so we were short of opponents and made up for it by playing against men's college sides, which was great fun. In our first match against a men's side, the bowler grinningly enquired if I wanted him to bowl underarm, to which I responded by hitting him for four! In the first match against female opposition, to my amazement, I was 84 not out – I had never scored more than fifteen before! I was very stiff the next day. I always preferred it if we fielded first because keeping wicket helped to get my eye in for batting.

In one match, I was keeping wicket when the batsman swung wildly and so late that he was actually facing me when he hit the ball – straight on to my arm, just above the glove. It was agony, and I thought it might be broken. That evening, I was at a party and was somewhat embarrassed by the fact that whenever I put out my hand to shake hands or take a glass of wine, my thumb would not stop twitching! But fortunately, it turned out that my arm was not broken.

Oxford had much more opportunity for cultural activities than I had had at home, with colleges putting on plays, concerts and other events quite cheaply, and the Oxford Playhouse was famous. I could not afford to go to the Playhouse often, but I could not resist the opportunity to see Marlene Dietrich, who must have been over sixty then. I was amazed. She was fantastic.

I was conscious of the so-called "Six-day War" in the Middle East, which shifted the balance of power and redrew boundaries, but I had no idea of the background, which stemmed from post-war period in 1948, when the UN partitioned the region into Jewish and Arab parts. The Arabs did not accept the partition, which they felt seized their ancestral land. Ever since then, there has been intermittent conflict in the region, and it is unresolved to this day.

When I went home for the holiday at the end of each term, I spent three weeks revising that term's work so that it was not too onerous to revise the whole year's work for the end of 1st year exams, known as prelims. It was compulsory to pass the prelims to continue to the 2nd year.

Chapter 7
Oxford 2nd Year

For the 2nd year, it was not possible to be in college, so the usual procedure was to find digs, but for scientists, there was an option to be in Cherwell Edge because it was close to the labs. It was actually a nunnery, but there was an agreement for St Hilda's to have twelve places there. It was rather strange living in a nunnery, but the sisters never ceased to amaze us with their lively humour. Again, we had to be in by ten thirty, but the door was manned by a senior student. My room was very pleasant, having windows on two sides with a window seat at each. One window looked over some college grounds, and American football was often played there, but I never managed to understand the rules.

St Hilda's today has several new buildings and has also been able to acquire other properties around Oxford, so that all students can be accommodated and, of course, it now accepts male students, having finally given up the all-women status in 2008.

In December 1967, Christiaan Barnard performed the first ever human heart transplant. The operation was successful, and the heart performed well, but the recipient lived for only eighteen days before succumbing to infection and pneumonia. In 1968 a recipient lived for 133 days. This was the problem at the beginning of transplant surgery: Immunosuppressant drugs had to be given to prevent rejection, but this left the patient vulnerable to infection. This was the dawn of the age; over the intervening years, techniques have improved; in particular, immunosuppressants have been developed which allow acceptance of the heart but do not leave the patient so vulnerable to infection. By 2002, over 50,000 transplants had been performed, and now transplants of a variety of different organs are routine.

We were amused at a fancy-dress party one evening to see the father of one of the students, a doctor, dressed as Dr Barnard.

Oxford is famous for its college balls. The five women's college balls were not quite as grand as the men's ones, but nonetheless attractive, and of course, for our own ball, it was our prerogative to issue the invitations. For the ball, night porters were engaged because the balls ended late, so the usual ten-thirty curfews did not apply, but for us, it was a problem. The accepted course of action was to swap rooms for the night with someone in college, but predictably, no one in college wanted to swap. One morning over breakfast, we were debating the difficulty, when I said, 'The shortest distance between two points is a straight line. We're not trying to do anything wrong; we have a right to go to the ball. Why don't we go and ask Mother Superior' – despite the fact that we had never even seen Mother Superior!

'Oh, what a good idea,' they all said, 'when are you going to see her?' I received a few days later. After I had explained the problem, she asked what time the ball finished.

I hedged a bit, not wanting to push my luck, but not wanting to sell the girls short and finally said, 'Oh, about four a.m.'

She thought for a moment or two, then said, 'I don't really see the problem – the doors here are opened at six thirty a.m. If you are going out, you may as well make a night of it.' The girls could not believe it.

Another morning over breakfast, I was bemoaning the lack of a Ballroom Dance Club since I had so enjoyed dancing. Yet again, I had let myself in for it because they all said, 'Start one then!' so I did. I found out what I would have to do to start a club and discovered that I could not associate it with the name of the university until it had been shown to be viable for some time. I also had to gain the support of a senior member of the university. That was harder said than done, even though I emphasised that we would do all the work and expect nothing of the senior member. Eventually, I found Dr Morrin Acheson, who was not only willing to be our senior member but was a ballroom dancer himself and wanted to be actively involved. He was a great support for many years. I had a few friends who were willing to help. The next step was a venue, and I eventually managed to arrange for us to use the top floor of the new Iffley Road sports stadium. We engaged the services of two local professional dance teachers and had a beginners' class in one room, while the intermediates practised in the other and then swapped over. It was quite hard work establishing the club at first, but I was delighted to see it develop to become one of the best-supported clubs in the university, with over a thousand members. I was lucky to be able to attend both the 10th and the 40th anniversary dances. It is now called Oxford University Dancesport Club and has many competitive events, including the annual match against Cambridge. Its website shows a wonderful picture of the present-day club and includes an article by Dr Acheson and one by me on the founding of the club.

Chapter 8
Camp Hiawatha

A common occupation for students for the summer holiday was to work in a summer camp in the USA. I applied and was accepted to Camp Hiawatha on the Maine/New Hampshire border. I believe that the fact that I was an Oxford blue had some influence – Americans are impressed. My mother was again very apprehensive. One of the things she said was, 'Make sure you take lots of insect repellent. You know they do everything twice as big in America.' She was right! The journey involved a flight to New York, then to Boston, then to a much smaller airfield and finally a pick-up to go to the camp. I made it without even losing my umbrella, but I was jetlagged for two days.

  We "counsellors" were there before the girls because the first couple of days, we were supposed to get things ready for the girls' arrival, such as putting the pontoons out on the lake to form the swimming area. In fact, it rained almost nonstop, so we didn't get much done and spent most of the time huddled around the huge open log fire in the main assembly room, smoking. Cigarettes were the equivalent of 2/6d per packet, so I'm afraid it did no good for my resolve not to smoke. Then the girls arrived, and the sun came out almost simultaneously. My tasks were to assist on the expeditions, canoeing, and some tennis. I vividly remember one canoe trip we took. We rode quite rough water, but then came to some rapids; the leader looked at it from above on a rock and pronounced that there was no way the girls could do it, so either we had to portage around the rapids, or she and I would have to take the canoes through one by one, loaded with all the equipment. I must admit she had more confidence in me than I had; however, we did make it.

Another trip was to Mt. Chocorua. We had hiked a long way and decided to camp just short of the summit so that we could get up early and see the dawn from the top. We did not have tents, just sleeping bags in the open. I had my bag tied closely around my face because my mother was right about the insects! I awoke in the dawn to find my face being licked by a raccoon, but it was worth it for the view from the top.

In the nearby boys' camp was a Puerto Rican tennis champion. He wanted to enter a local doubles tournament but had no partner. Someone suggested me, and he came over to practice with me. Obviously, I was no way near his standard, and I was terrified, but he was lovely and did not make me feel I was letting him down at all.

The highlight for the senior girls (seventeen-and eighteen-year-olds) was the trip north along the coast. We counsellors did not have to stay with the girls, so my colleague and I went to find a bar. We found what we thought looked a pleasant place, but a little while later it was raided by the police. We never did find out what they were after. When they found out we were British, the police were very nice to us and even bought us a drink but took us to the police station afterwards. It was then I remembered that the drinking age in this state was twenty-one not eighteen – my colleague was twenty-one, and I was twenty. I was about to confess before they looked at my passport when I remembered that in the US they put the month before the day, so they read my birthdate of 04/12/1947 as the 12 of April, which made me twenty-one. The treat for the girls on the way back was to stop for a meal of the famous Maine lobster. The portion included two whole lobsters! I had never eaten lobster, but I did manage to dissect the crustacean with the tools provided.

While we were at the camp, the real world intruded in the shape of the Vietnam War. One of the male counsellors received his draft papers and had to leave. The Vietnam War lasted almost twenty years from 1955. The USA supported South Vietnam against communist North Vietnam, backed by USSR and China, so it was really a proxy war between USA and USSR. Many Americans were against it and did not see why they should lose their young men. The USA had no real exit strategy.

At the end of the camp, I had three weeks to travel. I would have liked longer, but I felt I had to get back to do some work before starting the final year. It had turned out that my then boyfriend, before we knew each other, had also made arrangements to work in a summer camp, and several other friends had also independently made arrangements to work in the US, so we all met up. Three or four of them had rented a house in Schenectady and were working for General Electric. My friend John had asked the people in General Electric if he could bring a fellow physicist from Oxford to visit, but he failed to mention that it was a female, so when I turned up, they were somewhat surprised! My boyfriend, Chris, and I then went on to Canada to see Montreal, Niagara Falls and visit the site of the World Trade Fair, which was on the site of the Expo, which had taken place the year before. We finally all met up again in New York before flying home.

Chapter 9
Oxford 3rd Year

I was back in college. Goodbye, nuns. The focus for the 3rd year was study, but I made time for other activities too. I was captain of lacrosse, and since we had won the two previous Varsity matches against Cambridge, I was keen that we should make it three in a row. On paper, they were on the better side, but I told the girls the only way we could win was by being fitter than them. They said, 'OK, we'll all get super fit if you give up smoking!' so I agreed. On the day, I almost stood back on the sidelines shouting. 'You're great. Fantastic.' They played so well; we won.

During the Hilary term (Spring term), companies held interviews in the Randolph Hotel in Oxford for students who had applied for jobs with them, with the prospect of being invited to second interviews on site in the Easter holidays. I agonised over my first interview, worrying about how I would come across and trying to prepare answers to likely questions. When it came to it, they said, 'I'm sure our people in Sunderland would like to see you. We'll be in touch. Thank you.'

I said, 'Is that it?' I felt short-changed. In another interview, there were about six people (all men) doing the interview. Towards the end of the interview, I said, 'Do you usually have six senior people to interview one little graduate applicant? It doesn't seem a very effective use of time. I'm not sure I want to work for your company.'

They laughed and said, 'We all just wondered what you

looked like; a female lacrosse playing, cricketing, ballroom dancing physics graduate.'

So, I said, 'Oh, and who was right?'

They said, 'None of us!'

During the Easter holiday, I had interviews for jobs. The one in Sunderland was for Plessey Telecommunications. I went up by train – I did not know that you could travel for one and a half hours north of Sheffield and still be in England! I was put in a bed-and-breakfast overnight. The house had a huge picture window with a great view. I thought, *When you are two hundred miles from home, obey two rules: compliment your host and take an interest in the surroundings.* I said, 'Oh, what a beautiful view you have. What river is that?'

The host said, 'Wey aye, that's the North Sea, pet.' I did not know that Sunderland was on the coast.

I had an interview for the UKAEA (United Kingdom Atomic Energy Authority). I was told that if you got calculations wrong in one direction, it would cost the company a lot of money and your job; if you got it wrong in the other direction, it would irradiate three parts of Cheshire. I decided that, in the interest of the people of Cheshire, I should not accept the job.

During the Trinity term, finals were looming, but I made sure that I had scheduled all my revision so that I could afford to take time off and relax and enjoy Eights Week – the intercollege rowing event. It was traditional to support by "running the bank" shouting encouragement. In those days, none of the five female colleges had teams; even most of the men's colleges had only one team. It was not until 1981 that any woman took part in the annual boat race between Oxford and Cambridge, when Sue Brown from St Hilda's was appointed cox. Nowadays, all the colleges are mixed and most run several teams for both men and women. There is also a women's varsity boat race.

Close to the end of the last term at Oxford, it was customary for the principal to see each student to review the experience. I remember her asking what I thought I had learned most while at Oxford, and I said, 'How to make the most of each moment.'

She replied, 'Well, it is nice to see that our intuition paid off.' When I looked a little startled, she said, 'Your A-level grades and the material you wrote on your entrance papers didn't get you in here. We thought there was a spark worth developing, and you have proved that; you were never going to get a first, but you are a good, safe second, so you worked hard enough but left yourself with enough time to make the most of what Oxford has to offer.'

Exams were taken wearing "subfusc" academic dress consisting of a black skirt, white blouse, black tie (though most of us took liberties with the tie and had bows instead) and gown. It was a bit awkward for any Royal Navy personnel, who had to wear dress uniform, which included a sword! It was traditional, at the end of the exams, to go on a pub crawl, still in subfusc. My friend John and I were the only two of our group who were taking the atomic and nuclear optional paper, which was on Monday morning; everyone else finished on Saturday. We decided that we would celebrate with the rest of them on Saturday since we would have Sunday to recover. We drank drink for drink with everyone else and, at the end of the evening, when everyone else could hardly stand up, John and I looked at each other and realised we were both stone-cold sober. Obviously, despite our intentions, we had not been able to relax.

I can honestly say that in all my time at Oxford, I never experienced any hostile prejudice, neither because I was female, poorly taught or working class. Attitudes towards women were different then, but I did not find it difficult to cope with. In fact,

I relished the challenge.

Almost as soon as I was home for the summer holiday, came the historic Apollo 11 Moon landing. I sat up all night watching TV (we had a TV by then, but black and white). I loved the fact that Neil Armstrong repeated Galileo's hammer and feather experiment to show the effect of air resistance and assert that if there were no air resistance, then the hammer and feather would hit the ground at the same time. Galileo had to extrapolate because he could not remove air resistance altogether, but Armstrong could show it directly – there is no air on the Moon. The '60s have been called the decade of the Space Race, with the USSR and USA competing with each other to achieve various landmarks, though it had actually begun in the 1950s with the launch of the USSR's Sputnik, the first artificial satellite and first man-made object to orbit the Earth. The Space Race became an important symbol of superiority to whichever nation could lead. President JF Kennedy, in his famous speech in 1962, "We choose to go to the Moon," proposed landing a man on the Moon before 1970. The first spacecraft to impact the Moon's surface was USSR's Luna 2 in 1959. More unsuccessful missions followed until Ranger 7's provided the USA with close-up pictures of the Moon in 1964. USSR's Zond 3 did a flypast in 1965 and in 1966, Luna 9 did the first soft landing on the Moon. The first USA landing was Surveyor 1 also in 1966. Missions were becoming more and more reliable and successful on both sides, culminating in the Moon landing in 1969. Most people expected many more space missions, but though twelve men have walked on the Moon, the missions were all between 1969 and 1972.

At our graduation ceremony, I was standing in a group with my parents, Janet and her parents (also from Nuneaton) – all of us rather short. My friend John looked around the group and said,

'Ken Dodd got the wrong place!' This was a reference to Ken Dod's famous "Diddy Men" from Liverpool.

Shortly after we finished, Janet got married. I had made myself an outfit which consisted of a top, long waistcoat and skirt but also, as an alternative, a pair of "hot pants", which were all the rage. I reminded Janet that she would be looking at the photos long after hot pants had gone out of fashion and offered to be conservative and wear the skirt, but she insisted on the hot pants.

Chapter 10
Working at Plessey Telecommunications

I had intended to have a holiday before starting work, but a shortage of funds, desire to start my career, and a request from Plessey to begin as soon as possible persuaded me otherwise, and I began in September 1969. I set off for my new world on the train with £15 and a suitcase (trunk to follow). On arrival at the factory in Sunderland, the Personnel and Welfare department. (now known in most companies as HR – Human Resources dept.) arranged digs for me, and I was loaned £60 to be paid back at the rate of £20 for the next three months. My salary was to be £1500 per annum or 2000 depending on whether I had achieved a 2:2 or 2:1 degree. I tried to explain that Oxford did not differentiate between 2:1 and 2:2 and merely gave a 2, but they needed an answer, so finally my tutor wrote a letter saying it was top end of 2, not far off a first. I was not entirely convinced of that, but it got me the higher salary.

Plessey was a very large company with several divisions. The Telecommunications Division consisted of plants at Sunderland, South Shields, Liverpool and Beeston, Nottinghamshire. The Sunderland and South Shields plants were manufacturing equipment for telephone exchanges. When I asked for directions to the Plessey factory. I was greeted with blank stares, until someone said, 'Oh, you mean Erikson's' –

apparently, Plessey had taken over the site quite a few years earlier, but everyone still referred to it as Erikson's. I was on a graduate training scheme and joined the Training Department, which covered a vast range of different types of training activity such as wirers, mechanical engineers, maintenance engineers, clerical staff, quality control personnel, computer operators, financial staff and managers. We had a "Work Study Department" which was the latest idea to improve efficiency. They studied each operation and analysed it to determine the most efficient way of doing it. We had a computer room which was huge, and the data were input via punched cards. Punch-card operator was one of the key jobs, mainly performed by women. The data were stored on huge reels, which looked rather like film canisters.

There was only one other woman on the management team, who had been employed the year before. Eileen came from South Shields and was living at home with her parents, but she had been wanting to get her own flat, so she and I shared a flat in Washington New Town, just down the road from the factory, at the rate of £5 per month. She was in the Industrial Relations department. I had never learned to drive, whereas Eileen had a white Ford Anglia. She insisted on teaching me to drive, and my father sourced me an economical second-hand blue Anglia. We became famous for only having one car between us at any given time because one or other of them was usually off the road. We were trying to furnish the flat with second-hand buys and purchases from auctions; however, we decided it was not safe to buy a second-hand cooker and looked for hire purchase for a new one. We were turned down because we were women, despite both earning good salaries, but it could be done if Eileen's brother, who was eighteen and still at school, would act as guarantor! We were not amused.

For a time, I had a boyfriend in York. On one occasion, I was returning to Sunderland from the Midlands on the train, which passed through York, when I spotted him on the station. Imagine the surprise of everyone in the carriage, including me, when he leapt into the carriage, presented me with a box of Cadbury's Milk Tray and leapt off again just before the train pulled out. It was in imitation of a TV advert of the time: "All because the lady loves Milk Tray". I wondered how he knew which train I was on but learned later that he had met every train from the Midlands that day.

At some time, we had another girl, Liz, to share the flat (I can't remember why!) It was not a great decision. Eileen and I had never had strict rules about the flat-share; it had just seemed obvious, but with Liz, it didn't work that way. She worked for the local authority developing "Washington New Town" and as part of creating a community, she was to start a Guide Company. I said I would help when I could, but she must not rely on me; it was her responsibility. Of course, that didn't happen; she was frequently unavailable, but I couldn't let the girls down when she was not there. We had some memorable events, including a fashion show and a "Thinking Day" celebration. One of the most rewarding occasions was when the mother of one of the girls knocked on the door. She was almost crying and said how grateful she was. Apparently, she had been worried that her daughter was getting in with some doubtful company but knew that if she banned her from seeing them, it would just make her more determined. Now, when they called to see her, she just said, 'Oh, not now. I have better things to do.'

At Plessey, I was allotted various tasks, including devising an induction programme for new employees. The only available visual aid technique was a white board with cards backed with magnetic strips, so I spent a lot of time drawing and writing the cards. Later I was sent on a course to learn how to make the most of the latest technique – overhead projector slides.

We had what was called "The twilight shift" for wirers. Wiring was a skilled and well-paid job. It involved connecting a whole array of pins together with various coloured wires according to a given pattern. It had been found that women were much better at it than men, probably because they are more dextrous (as a left-hander, I do object that the word "dextrous" comes from the Latin for "right" and that the word for "left" is "sinister" – but I digress). The twilight shift was very popular with married women because their husbands could look after the children, removing the need for childcare. At one time, a local factory called "Cigarette Components" had closed down, so there were lots of women looking for jobs, and their jobs at Cigarette Components had involved a similar need for dexterity. They were ideal candidates for the twilight shift, and we had hundreds of applicants, but there was one essential qualification: they must not be colour-blind. This was not just because they would make mistakes, it was not good for their own eye health, nonetheless, some were so desperate for a job, they would try to cheat the "Ischihara" tests which we used. This test consisted of a series of sheets of dots of different colours with a number in another colour in the centre. Friends who had done the test would tell them the sequence of the numbers so that they could get them right, but we defeated the cheats by randomly inserting a sheet which had no numbers on it at all.

At one time, I was given the role of liaison with a team of consultants who were to carry out a Job evaluation exercise for the whole workforce at the two sites, Sunderland and South

Shields. The aim was to set up a sophisticated evaluation of all the jobs (some 2000 of them) and rank them so that when future pay rises were considered, the structure remained the same; only the overall level had to be negotiated, which should make pay negotiations easier. We had three different Trade Unions, but the South Shields site came under a different regional branch from Sunderland, so it was effectively six unions. I was not intimidated by the thought of unions or shop stewards; my father had been a shop steward for the Union of Sheet Metal Workers and later a branch secretary. On the whole, we had good relationships with them, especially the Works Convenor, Nick (the overall coordinator).

The first stage of the process was an opinion poll, the main purpose of which was to get the cooperation and involvement of the workforce, rather than them seeing it as being imposed on them. The results were analysed by computer, but in those days, that only went as far as producing streams of paper with punched holes at the side with a series of 0s and 1s. We had to check the whole stream, which was a very tedious task, and it was difficult to stay focused. Then we had to convert the numbers into percentage answers for each question. After the opinion poll, the real work of classifying the jobs began. All jobs had to have a written job description agreed by the employee, and then negotiations with the unions ranked the jobs against criteria such as difficulty, danger, skill, experience, etc. It took a long time to reach an agreement. Some jobs met with almost universal agreement, such as engineer, maintenance engineer and toolmaker as the top three jobs; others were more difficult. The jobs were then grouped into about five bands. The idea was that once the bands were agreed, at any future wage negotiation there would be no change in individual jobs, merely agreement on the pay associated with each band. There also had to be an agreed appeals procedure and dispute procedure. It took a long time and demanded goodwill on all sides.

I eventually became engaged to Edwin, one of the consultants. In late 1970, he was deployed to another job in Africa. I had already been having second thoughts about the engagement, but he had booked me a trip to visit him in Dar es Salam and Nairobi over Christmas. When I was at home, friends kept saying, 'Oh, you must be so excited', when in fact I was dreading it, but felt that I owed it to Edwin to talk about it face-to-face. I agonised over whether to tell him as soon as I landed that I had decided to call off the engagement, in which case the next fortnight would be difficult, or leave it until later. In fact, it could be read all over my face when I got off the plane. I never was any good at dissembling. It was a strange holiday, quite aside from the agonies of breaking up. His company had been engaged to make a study of the usage of the port at Dar es Salam and predict necessary future development. The house where we stayed had a cook/housekeeper who lived in a mud hut at the bottom of the garden. I found it very difficult to cope with giving orders for meals etc, but if he had not had the job, he and his family would have starved. I had never encountered anything like it before, but I could not see how it was possible to change the situation overnight. The authorities at the time were insisting that companies begin to replace foreign managers with local ones, so there were a number of managers (mainly Scots, it seemed) who were training local workers to do their jobs before returning to the UK. It seemed surreal to be doing Scottish country dancing in the extreme heat on New Year's Eve. As I returned to the UK. Edwin was still trying to persuade me not to break off the engagement.

These were difficult times. There was much inequality in Africa, even though the apartheid system mainly applied to South Africa. In theory, it was about separate development (Apartheid means "separate" in Afrikaans), but in practice it enabled the white, twenty per cent minority, mainly of Dutch origin, to dominate and discriminate against other racial groups socially, politically, educationally, economically and almost any other conceivable way. Non-white groups were not allowed to vote, hold office, open businesses, or engage in professional practices. There were separate "white-only" areas in all kinds of facilities, beaches, shops and schools; there were even white-only ambulances. The non-white facilities were always inferior to the white ones. Nelson Mandela had been associated with the African Nationalist Congress (ANC) and supported a campaign of protest against apartheid, initially non-violent, but later he instigated a campaign of sabotage. He had been prosecuted several times between 1956–1961 for "Acts of Sedition", but in 1962, he had been arrested and charged with conspiracy to overthrow the state and sentenced to life imprisonment. He was imprisoned for twenty-seven years.

In December 1970, on my birthday, Eileen had arranged a surprise party for me because, with Edwin in Africa, I had not done anything socially for two months. She had lots of our friends making food and hiding it all over the place. She got me to do my makeup and hair and get party dressed by saying, 'Look, you've not done anything for ages, I'll do some food, you dress up and we'll pretend we're going out.' One of the guests was an associate of Liz at the local authority, Robert, an engineer. I think it was fortuitous because if I hadn't known that there was the possibility of a new relationship, I might not have had the courage to hold out for cancelling the engagement to Edwin and;

as it turned out, that would have been a mistake.

Shortly after I came back from Africa, there was a postal strike for seven weeks, which caused considerable disruption in a time before mobiles, emails, texts, WhatsApp and when not every household had a 'phone. The telephone was not considered secure or recordable, so all official business was conducted by letter. It coincided with decimalisation and compounded the difficulty with the changeover. Apparently, the motivation for the change was to simplify financial transactions and reduce mistakes in calculation. No doubt, young people had no difficulty switching, but many older people never did get used to 100p in a pound, instead of 12d to a shilling, 20 shillings to a pound, sixpences and three-penny bits. There were moves for metrication as well, but it didn't actually become compulsory. I had no difficulty accepting the metric (metres, kilometres, grams and kilograms) as opposed to imperial (feet, inches, pounds and ounces), since we had been taught imperial but had to use metric in science.

Most people were unaware of the 1971 "Immigration Act", which gave permanent right to remain to any people from British colonies who were already living in the UK by that date (obviously including the Windrush generation), but it would become a big problem for many people in the future.

At this time, I was only vaguely aware of the conflict in India, which led to the creation of Bangladesh, and certainly knew nothing of the historical issues, but that would change much later when I met my second husband, who had spent time in Pakistan.

In February, my flatmate Eileen went skiing (I decided I couldn't afford it). She met a number of people, including Ben, a Dutchman, who worked for C and A, based in Liverpool and

Sunderland, and John Bradshaw, a salesman for Rumenco, an animal feed manufacturer, based in Burton-on-Trent. John was celebrating his decree nisi, so there was quite a party. When everyone returned home, John was promoted to Regional Sales Manager and moved to the North East, so he decided to look up the friends he had made skiing. Ben was unavailable, so the next on the list was Eileen. They met for a drink and ended up in the same pub where I was with Rob. Apparently, John said, 'I like the flatmate; pity about the boyfriend.'

Eileen replied, 'Don't worry; he's emigrating to Canada in a month's time.' Rob had always wanted to go to Canada and had been making plans when we met. We talked about my going with him, but it didn't work out that way. Friends joked about what I did to men to send them to far-flung places: Chris went to Abu Dhabi after university, Edwin went to Africa, and now Rob was going to Canada. Sure enough, a month later, John phoned to ask for a date.

1971 was the year of the Industrial Relations Act. Its aim was to stabilise industrial relations by concentrating responsibility for negotiation with the trade unions using the courts. Special courts called "industrial tribunals" were to be set up, consisting of a trade union representative, a management representative and a legally qualified chairman. The original intention was that no lawyers should be involved. This was a complete departure in industrial relations, where there had never been any legislation. Part of my responsibilities was to train the managers on the changes they would have to make to their procedures to comply with the Act, e.g. new definitions of "unfair dismissal" and procedures for warnings before a final dismissal. There was dissention on the part of the trade unions because it eroded same of their traditional powers, although it gave more rights to individual workers. The Act was repealed in 1974 and replaced by the Trade Union and Labour Relations Act.

1972 saw the miners' strike. Competition with cheap oil imports meant the coal industry was struggling with increasing losses, and the miners' wages had not kept up with other industrial workers. Since the 1960s, the policy of the National Coal Board had been to concentrate on the most profitable pits, which meant closures and reduced numbers of miners. The problem was compounded because some towns and villages were totally dependent on the industry, leaving them devasted if there was a closure. Despite the closures, the industry was still losing money, leading to pressure to keep wage increases low. Miners had gone from being twenty-two per cent above the average for other industries to being two per cent below.

The strike was characterised by the union sending "flying pickets" to other industrial sites to persuade other workers to strike in solidarity, which led to railway workers and power station employees refusing to handle coal. A state of national emergency was declared, amid widespread power cuts; sometimes lasting up to four hours duration. It was not too bad during daylight hours as it was possible to read or play board games or cards – remember, there were no games consoles or Kindles – but if it was dark, there was little for it but to go to bed. The dispute became more violent with police involved more often after a miner was killed on the picket line when a non-union lorry driver mounted the pavement to pass the line. Finally, after seven weeks, an agreement was reached, but that point marked the beginning of the decline of the mining industry.

One Sunday, we were relaxing in our flat watching *How Green Was My Valley* on TV. I was lying with my head in John's lap. When I tried to get up at the end of the film, I yelled out in pain. Everyone thought I was joking, but I was in agony. The next morning, my boss was due to pick me up to go to the Liverpool factory, leaving very early. I struggled out of bed but could go no further and retreated (remember, there were no mobile phones, so I could not let him know). He apparently waited downstairs for a while, then left for Liverpool; he was so busy in meetings. He did not check on me and assumed I had overslept and was in work in South Shields. Eileen, meanwhile, assumed I was in Liverpool. It was some time before people realised I was in neither place and must still be in bed and called a doctor. He said he thought it was a kidney infection and prescribed medication, but half an hour later, he was back with an ambulance, saying he would not take the risk, and I found myself in Gateshead General Hospital. It was definitely a kidney problem, but they were not sure if it was an infection or stones. I was given all sorts of medication, and they scheduled an IVP (an intravenous pyelogram), but it took a week before it occurred.

One evening, I noticed the load of pills was different from before. The nurse said, 'It's OK, they're different each time,' but I was suspicious and hesitated.

A couple of minutes later, she rushed over and said, 'Have you taken those pills?'

When I said I hadn't, she said, 'Thank goodness, they're for the lady over there. These are yours.'

I asked what the lady was in for, and the answer was a hysterectomy! The IVP was a very strange experience. A radioactive liquid was injected and allowed to flow around the body. It felt as if I was glowing, possibly giving off a green light! Apparently, it shows up the activity of the kidneys. By now, the medication had done its work, or if there were stones, they had been passed, so all was fine and I never did find out which it was;

however, the aftermath was three months during which my blood count was so low I caught every infection going and was off work most of the time.

Part of John's area of responsibility was Northern Ireland, and this was the time of the troubles, so I was very worried every time he had to go there. The violent sectarian struggles emanated from the fact that the, mainly protestant, loyalists wanted NI to remain part of the UK, whereas the catholic republicans wanted NI to become part of Eire. The Catholics were a minority and felt deprived by the authorities. The Irish Republican Army (The IRA) viewed it as a guerrilla war for national independence, whereas the unionist parliamentary forces viewed it as terrorism. Over the years of the conflict, which was not resolved until 1998, some 3,600 people were killed and over 30,000 wounded. There were bombings, street fighting, sniper attacks and revenge killings, and it was not confined to Northern Ireland. There were bombings in London too.

In Uganda, Idi Amin became the dictator, following a coup. He promised elections, saying, "I am a soldier, not a politician." but as time went on, it became apparent that that would not happen. At first, other world leaders embraced him; Western leaders were pleased with anything other than a communist regime. It soon became apparent that he was a monster. He was arrogant and cruel. He became an absolute tyrant and a murderer, disposing violently of anyone who threatened his rule or displeased him. The number of people killed is estimated at between 100,000 and 300,000. He expelled Asians and Europeans and took over their businesses, which then failed. It was his overarching arrogance which finally finished his regime in 1979 when he invaded Tanzania. He fled to Libya and then to Saudi Arabia. He was never tried for his crimes.

John took me to our favourite Italian Restaurant in Newcastle, and to the accompaniment of a violinist, proposed. We started looking for a house and ended up purchasing a new build in Sherrif Hutton, a village north of York. The price was £8000, which meant a mortgage of £66 per month; our friends thought we were mad to take on such a financial burden. I recognised that it would be difficult to have a worthwhile marriage and a career in industry (there was no support in those days – no maternity leave, no concessions on hours, little nursery provision), so I sought a teaching job. Later, it would have been necessary to take a year's teaching course, but at that time, a degree was considered sufficient, with two years' probation before being declared a qualified teacher. These were the days of "gazumping". Because the demand outstripped supply, builders or vendors would agree on a price, then just before contracts were signed, if another buyer came along with a higher offer, sell to them instead or get into a leapfrogging auction. It was very disturbing. We felt we had narrowly escaped it when we went to see "our" house to discover that the bathroom was pink, not blue, as we requested. It turned out that it was not a mistake; the builder was undecided whether to sell to us or another buyer.

In early September, during the Summer Olympics of that year, the terrorist group "Black September" murdered eleven members of the Israeli team in Munich.

Chapter 11
Teaching at Manor House School

1973 was the year that the United Kingdom, along with Denmark and the Republic of Ireland joined the European Economic Community (E.E.C.), later to become the European Union.

We moved to Ashby-de-la-Zouch in the summer, but could not move into our house immediately, so we were in a tiny, rented, 1-up-1 down, on a corner where the road took a ninety-degree turn. Heavy lorries used to grind up the hill and round the corner. It was awful; I would close all the windows to shut out the noise and fumes, but after ten minutes, I could not stand the stuffiness, so I would have to open them again. This sequence went on all day. The house next door had had lumps knocked off the roof by lorries several times. I had to spend two days cleaning the kitchen before I dared cook anything. The toilet was in a shed at the bottom of the yard, so going out for a drink at night was not recommended. I didn't know houses like that still existed; even less that they could be put up for rent. Modern regulations would not allow it.

Manor House School catered for boys up to thirteen, for the Common Entrance exam to public schools and girls up to eleven for the 11+ exam to local schools.

As Head of Science, I could dictate the syllabus, so I decided on the first three years of Nuffield physics, chemistry and biology. The Nuffield scheme was a new approach relying heavily on practical work and learning from experiments. My laboratory was a lean-to greenhouse against a wall, which got very hot in summer and cold in winter, but being able to teach the Nuffield syllabus more than made up for the discomfort. The biology syllabus included breeding and studying locusts and pomatoceros triqueter – a marine worm – with which, under a microscope, it is possible to actually see the sperm and eggs joining.

The girls had not really done any games, and there was no tarmac area big enough for a netball court, but I decided we could manage on a 2/3 length court; in fact, it was good for the girls because if they managed to be organised on the small court, they found it much easier on a full-sized court. I set about getting them a team kit and organising matches with local schools – in fact, they played against my old school. By the end of their second term, the girls beat a local school who had just won the County championship. In the summer term, we did rounders, and again the girls were so keen; it was very satisfying to teach them.

I ran a gymnastics after-school club, doing the BAGA (British Amateur Gymnastics Award) scheme for schools. The boys and girls loved doing a display on Sports day.

In 1974, Richard Nixon, President of the USA, finally resigned after being impeached over the "Watergate Scandal", which had been going on since 1972. The events had unfolded gradually following a break-in at the Democratic National Committee headquarters in the Watergate Office building in Washington D.C. It emerged that President Nixon had sanctioned attempts to cover up his party's involvement in the break-in. Nixon attempted to resist investigations but was finally forced to hand over tapes from the Oval Office, which demonstrated his complicity. It was revealed that his aides had been guilty of bugging political opponents' offices and the misuse of government agencies for political purposes, among other illicit operations.

The whole of the UK was both fascinated and revolted by the saga of Lord Lucan. A former Coldstream Guardsman, he was married with children, but a known gambler who often lost more than he won and had a liking for the high life, driving an Aston Martin and racing power boats. His marriage collapsed in 1972, and he lost custody of his children and moved out of the family home. In 1974, the children's nanny was murdered. Lucan maintained that he had surprised an assailant attacking his wife, but she claimed Lucan had killed the nanny and attacked her. Later, Lucan drove off and his car, complete with bloodstains and other incriminating evidence, was found abandoned in Newhaven. An inquest into the nanny's death named Lucan as the killer, but he has never been found and was declared officially dead in 1999.

I was surprised one day to come home to find a policeman on the doorstep. He wanted to talk to John. I suppose everyone feels the same – even though you know you have done nothing wrong, you feel a certain trepidation. The police wanted to know where John had been and what cars he had access to over a prolonged period, which was a tall order since, being a Sales Manager, he drove many different company cars and travelled a lot. We were confounded, until the policeman explained that John had been in a Rugby club years before, in which there were associates of Donald Neilson. The police had hit a brick wall in their investigations and had gone right back to questioning all known associates, however loosely connected. Donald Neilson, dubbed "The Black Panther" by the press, was wanted for armed robbery and murder and finally for the kidnap of Lesley Whittle, the daughter of a wealthy businessman. Neilson had attempted to blackmail her father, but the exchange of money by her brother was bungled and she ultimately died at the bottom of a drainage shaft, possibly killed accidentally by the tether round her neck. Nielson was finally caught, convicted and sentenced to life in prison.

When I went to the doctor to find out if I was pregnant, the first thing he said, to my surprise, was "What size shoes do you take?" He explained that the size of the hip girdle is related to shoe size and that at my height (5 feet 2 inches) if I had shoe size 2 or 3 instead of 5, I might have had to have a caesarean to give birth. Everyone remembers the summer of 1976, which was one of the hottest on record, but 1975 was nearly as bad. Pregnant women were not as well catered for then in terms of clothing, equipment, gadgets etc. I remember I eventually found a swimsuit designed for pregnant women, and being in a pool, with the weight supported by the water, was bliss. Being short and with a rapidly increasing bust, I found it hard to find clothing which didn't make me look like a tent. The most flattering outfit was a pair of specially designed trousers, with an elasticated front panel, and a matching top, which I made. Towards the end of my pregnancy, we were due to go to a Company dinner/dance. I tried to replicate the trouser outfit in velvet, but it was not elegant enough, so I was delighted when I came across a full-length black chiffon "handkerchief" dress in a local shop – it had triangular pieces of chiffon delicately draped and was very flattering. The assembled group of ladies, standing chatting with me at the dinner/dance, were highly amused when one of the salesmen – presumably ignorant of the fact that I was not only the boss's wife, but also eight months pregnant – started chatting me up.

Chapter 12
Post Timothy

Timothy Giles Stewart Bradshaw was born on 21 October 1975. He was three weeks early and was "face-to-pubes", i.e. looking up instead of down, which apparently presents a bigger circumference. Although the birth began well, it stalled, and I had to have suction (I doubt they do that anymore), tore and was cut, so I needed about forty-five stitches. The stitches made it painful to sit, so I did not manage to breastfeed, but nonetheless, Tim thrived. He slept little, was on his feet by six months old and walked independently at nine months. Nowadays, he would be diagnosed as having ADHD – being hyperactive – but it was unheard of in those days. I suffered from severe postnatal depression, but it was not recognised then. The doctor told me to just get on with it and be grateful I had a healthy baby. Men took a different attitude towards babies too. It was not the norm to be at the birth or to be very hands-on. John never changed a nappy or fed Tim.

At the time, I was driving an NSU – a rear-engined car. One day, when I had driven over to Nuneaton to see my mother, I had to pause to exit a carpark. I glanced in the rear window and was horrified to see flames coming from the engine. Tim was just lying in his carrycot on the back seat, looking up at the flames and giggling. I usually had difficulty getting the carrycot out of the back because it got tangled in the seat belt, but I don't even remember trying. The next minute, I was standing on the pavement with the cot in my hands. A shopkeeper came out with a fire extinguisher and put out the flames, but a little later they flared up again. I was terrified the car would explode. A police motorcyclist stopped and finally managed to put out the flames. He was concerned that I was blocking the exit from the carpark and said, 'Back it up a bit.'

I said, 'Are you seriously asking me to get in that car and turn the ignition on?' He got in, much to the consternation of all of us, but it did not catch fire again, and he backed up. The shopkeeper let me use his phone, and my dad came and drove the car to his mechanic friend. Pete said it was a minor fault with the timing of the ignition, and he fixed it, but I could never bring myself to get in the car again, and we sold it immediately. I was appalled that a "minor fault" could cause a car to catch fire.

When Tim was about five months old, he was in a "walker" – a device with little wheels on the end of a metal frame which he used to race around. His father was supposed to be keeping an eye on him, but even though I warned him how fast Tim could move, John was unprepared. Tim hurtled across the patio, over the edge and tipped head-first into the onions. He came up covered in soil; that was when I decided that it was no longer necessary to sterilise everything he touched! He used to climb up and over everything. We nicknamed him "Unimog" after a toy truck of the time, which was not stopped by anything – it just went up and over it. I joked that either he or I would not survive to his fifth birthday. I was permanently tired.

Ashby-de-la-Zouch was twinned with a French town, and since John was playing rugby for the local side, he suggested inviting the French rugby team to visit. It was duly arranged, and the team was to stay with the Ashby families. Since the French players did not speak much English and the English did not speak much French, that could have been tricky. So, John decided the French group should all come to us for a get-together party as soon as they arrived. The other wives all offered to help with the preparations, to which I said, 'No point until seven thirty p.m. when Tim goes to bed, but then, yes please, all hands on deck'. The coach duly pulled up on our drive. The evening passed in a whirl. I was in the kitchen most of the time, but thought that considering hardly anyone spoke each other's language, there was an awful lot of noise! The wine seemed to be flowing freely, which probably contributed to the jollity. I was bemused until one of the Frenchmen grabbed me by the hand and took me out to the back of the coach to point out a couple of barrels of wine, complete with taps!

A colleague of John's encouraged him to join an organisation called the "British Junior Chamber" which was an organisation for young businessmen focused on self-development and service to the local community. John was very quickly nominated social secretary, so there were lots of events. One evening, when we were having a social evening at a local hotel, I asked if women were allowed to join the Chamber. The men looked a bit nonplussed but said they didn't think there was anything in the rules against women joining; it was just that there were no women members. For quite a long time, I was the only woman member of Burton-on-Trent Junior Chamber.

One Saturday, I was pushing Tim in his pushchair when I realised that the Ashby Ladies Hockey team would be playing and decided to go and watch. I had played with the team before having Tim, but John played rugby, and I could not find a regular babysitter for a Saturday. I stood chatting to the goalkeeper when she said, 'Why aren't you out there, we need you.' When I explained she said, 'My daughter always comes to watch; she will happily push Tim around the touchline.' I was delighted. I did manage to get a babysitter for the County Championships. Ashby Ladies was a lovely club; we played seriously, but not too seriously, so it was fun. We had no great aspirations for the Championships because teams like Leicester Ladies took it all very seriously indeed and had lots of players who were internationals. I told the babysitter that I would be back by lunchtime because we did not expect to get out of the group stages, but in fact, I had to 'phone her several times as we progressed and found ourselves in the final against Leicester Ladies. It was a 1-1 draw at full-time and still after extra time. The method for deciding the winner was "territorial advantage" – how long each team had spent in the opposition's half. We lost by two minutes. I think modern soccer would benefit from this system instead of the lottery of penalties, and it would also encourage teams to be more attacking rather than passing back.

Chapter 13
Post Stephen

I wasn't at all sure that I could survive another child, but decided that it wasn't possible to have another like Tim and settled on giving it until Tim was two. If I wasn't pregnant by then, we would not have any more children. In the meantime, John had changed his job, and we had moved to Wolverhampton. We now live in a large five-bedroomed house with two-thirds acre of garden. The next-door neighbours asked us if they could hold their daughter's wedding in a marquee on our lawn, and we agreed. The large house also proved a boon for the street party for the Queen's Silver Jubilee.

Somewhat surprisingly, John's company, Midland Shires Farmers, was the biggest customer of Texaco, which sponsored James Hunt in F1 racing and Barry Sheene in motorcycle racing – both World Champions that year. It turned out that the car and the bike appeared at the Midland Shires Farmers stand at the Farmers' Show, and there is a photo of Tim astride the bike.

In fact, I was pregnant by June 1977, so Stephen Charles Stewart Bradshaw was born in February 1978. This time the birth was swift, but Stephen had a high bilirubin count, so we had to stay in the hospital for a while.

One day, not long before Christmas, I took a phone call and was surprised to hear a voice speaking French. It was Suzanne saying that she and her husband Michel were coming to London shopping and could they come and see us! The visit was a great success, and Suzanne and Michel could not get enough of the leg of Welsh lamb which I served.

1978 saw an amazing development in fertility treatment with the birth of the first so-called "test tube baby". In vitro fertilization involves removing egg cells from the mother, fertilising them directly with sperm in a test tube or petri dish, then reintroducing the embryo into the womb. At the time, it was controversial; there were many practical and ethical issues. It was impossible to be sure if the child would develop normally. In fact, Louise Brown is a doctor, is married and has two children born naturally. Nowadays, the procedure is common, and millions of test-tube babies have been born.

For most of the twentieth Century, Iran and the USA enjoyed close relations; the CIA even helped the Shah, the hereditary leader, to stay in power against a coup. However, many Iranians saw the Shah as corrupt and in 1979, the Islamic Revolution brought Ayatollah Khomeini to power as the religious leader of the new Islamic State. Shortly afterwards students laid siege to the American Embassy in Tehran. I remember both of these events being broadcast on the news. Diplomatic relations have still not been restored.

At this time, I took a part-time job teaching at a sixth form college in Smethwick.

At sixty-two, my mother had never had a day off work ill, but she began to feel unwell and after a couple of misdiagnoses was told she had leukaemia; she deteriorated rapidly and there was nothing more they could do.

Meanwhile, we had moved to a smaller, more modern house in Bridgnorth. The move added quite a lot of time and distance onto my commute to Smethwick. On the day we moved in, I took the first call on the newly connected phone. It was the hospital telling me that my mother had about four days to live. Two days after my mother died, John told me he had been having an affair and wanted a divorce. Psychologists say that the top events for stress are: the death of a close relative; divorce; changing job and moving house. I had had all of them in the space of a few weeks.

There are no words to express how I felt at that time.

Part 2

Chapter 14
Move to Worcester

My husband did not go through with the divorce at this time. His girlfriend lived with her parents, so their getting together would require a commitment to buy or rent a new property. I firmly believe that if she had a place of her own, he would have left me and just moved in with her. I was devastated. I knew I had not been much fun for some time, because I found it very hard with an ADHD four-year-old and a two-year-old. I rarely had more than four hours sleep a night and was permanently tired. In those days, men were not expected to be hands-on, and John had never changed a nappy or fed either of the boys. In fact, I was suicidal, but it would be the boys who found me in the morning, and I could not countenance that.

Remarkably, my friend Janet, with whom I had actually been at primary school, high school and also at Oxford, phoned me out of the blue. Since university, we had gone our separate ways; Janet had been studying law and was now a lawyer in London. I had gone to the North East to work in Plessey. Although we still sent each other cards, we were not frequently in touch, so it was astounding that she should ring just then. She invited me to take the boys to London to stay with her for the weekend. It was a great solace, but I left it rather late on the Sunday before setting off to drive home on the M1. Stephen had been crying for some time in the car seat in the back. I'm not sure what happened exactly, but the next thing I knew I hit the crash barrier and bounced back across two lanes to finish in a coned-off section of the hard shoulder. Remarkably, no one hit me. The car seemed OK, but I did not know if I had caused any serious damage, other than the imprint of the barrier all along the side of the car. At least, Stephen had stopped crying! I sat wondering what to do when I noticed the road sign showed that Nuneaton was the next junction, so I nursed the car to my parents' house. Dad checked the car and proclaimed only bodywork damage, so I drove home the next day.

John changed his job again, and we moved to a pleasant three-bedroomed detached house in Worcester and tried to put things right – at least I did; I'm not convinced he ever tried very hard. In September, Tim started at Sunnyside, a small independent school in Worcester. When we visited the school, the pupils were practising for a poetry competition. I was impressed with their confidence, recall and presentation, but hoped that there was not too much emphasis on rote learning. The uniform list included a tracksuit, which was kept in school for the week. I thought it a bit over-the-top, until I discovered the reason: there was no tarmac playground, the boys went to play at the racecourse, which was usually muddy. The tracksuit practically walked home by itself at the end of the week!

In 1980, six armed Iranian Arabs stormed the Iranian Embassy in London and took twenty-six hostages, including staff, visitors, and a policeman. They were demanding the release of prisoners in Khuzestan and safe passage out of the UK. Five hostages were released for minor concessions, but on the sixth day, the gunmen killed a hostage and threw his body out of the embassy. The operation was handed over to the army, and the SAS carried out a raid, which was transmitted live on TV. It lasted seventeen minutes, and all but one of the hostages were rescued and all but one of the gunmen were killed. In the following years, until 1984, Colonel Gaddafi ordered the deaths of a number of exiled opponents in London and Manchester. It culminated in 1984 with the death of policewoman Yvonne Fletcher, who was killed by a bullet fired from the Iranian embassy during an anti-Gaddafi protest. Eleven Iranians were also killed. Most people's reaction was outraged that innocent lives should be lost in our country because of their disputes. Diplomatic relations were broken with Iran. In retaliation, six British nationals were arrested in Iran but released nine months later. Ayatollah Khomeini declared that the fate of the fifty-three American Embassy hostages taken by armed students in 1979 would be decided by the Iranian parliament. They were released in 1981.

The USA boycotted the Summer Olympics in Moscow in protest at the Soviet invasion of Afghanistan the previous year. This was yet another proxy war which continued through the '80s. Many years later, Tim was to serve two tours in Afghanistan with the Honourable Artillery Company of the British army.

The GPS (Global Positioning System) project had been started in the 1970s by the US Department of Defense. The first prototype satellite was launched in 1978, and by 1980, further operational satellites were in place. Although the US government created, controls and maintains the system, it is freely available to anyone. At first, it was mainly used by the military, civil and commercial users. Today, it is ubiquitous and an essential part of many other facilities.

We were all familiar with Radio Caroline. A "pirate radio station". It had been set up in 1964, based on a ship off the coast, to circumvent the BBC's radio broadcasting monopoly and the record companies' control of popular music broadcasting. In

1980, the *Mi Amigo*, the ship of that time, sank in a storm. It was replaced in 1983. Altogether, five different ships were used. Very recently, I saw Tony Blackburn, one of the first DJs, on TV.

1981 saw the launch of the first Space Shuttle. This was a key point in the history of space exploration because the shuttle was reusable. It opened up a new era of missions. Over the next thirty years, shuttles would take people into orbit, launch, repair and recover satellites, and build the International Space Station. Cutting edge research would vastly increase our understanding of space.

This was also the year in which the Greenham Common protest began. A group of Welsh women called "Women for life on Earth" marched to the RAF base at Greenham Common to protest against the government allowing Cruise nuclear missiles to be stored at the base. They realised they would need more publicity than just the march, and so they began camping outside the gates. The camp became well established, with some women living there with their children. It became an almost permanent feature and was not finally dismantled until 2000.

After much press speculation, the blossoming relationship between Prince Charles and Lady Diana Spencer culminated in an engagement and, later in the same year, the grand spectacle of the Royal Wedding. Everyone saw it as a fairy-tale romance.

Steve joined Tim at Sunnyside. I answered an advertisement for a part-time chemistry teacher at The Alice Ottley School, an independent secondary school for girls. Apparently, the headmistress was delighted because, although her immediate need was for a chemistry teacher, she was conscious that she had no cover for physics. So, although I began by teaching chemistry, I was soon teaching physics. For O-level, the girls had the choice of physics or Latin, and since most of them were confident of passing Latin, but not so physics, they opted for Latin – until I convinced them otherwise!

I was teaching chemistry to a group of girls who were preparing to take the 16+ exam. This was a certificate for pupils who might struggle with GCE O-level and would otherwise take the CSE (Certificate of Secondary Education). However, this exam allowed for some overlap, in that, if a pupil scored a 1 at CSE it would be a C (or possibly even higher) in O-level. The CSE results would come out first, and then if any of them were a 1, it would appear on the O-level list. The first year, my head of department was very pleased that one of my pupils achieved a 1 at CSE, which became a C at O-level. The next year, I had five with 1s and waited anxiously for the O-level lists. My head of department said, 'Oh, don't get excited; they won't be more than a C.' Three of them received Bs. I was delighted. The syllabus included a discussion of the increasing use of plastics and an awareness that the difference between traditional materials and plastics is that plastic is non-biodegradable, meaning it does not break down naturally and so can cause a disposal problem as has become all too obvious today.

This was the start of a period of experimentation with exams; the aim was to establish a single exam for all pupils, but of course, this is very difficult with a large range of ability, exams which less able pupils can cope with do not differentiate between pupils of higher ability. This is especially true of subjects like maths and science. The final outcome was the GCSE exam, introduced in 1985, but it still had to retain some differentiation in having different "tiers" to achieve the full range of ability.

I looked for a Junior Chamber in Worcester but was disappointed to find that the nearest one was in Kidderminster. I attended a few meetings, but it was really too far away. Someone suggested that there should be a Chamber in Worcester and that I should start it, so I did. I found a good core of enthusiastic people, and we set it up. For one of the early Monday speaker meetings, I thought it would be interesting to have someone from the police to talk about forensic science. Unfortunately, apart from an interesting bit about fingerprints, the policeman who came seemed to be interested only in shocking us with pictures. In 1973, David McGreavy, dubbed the Monster of Worcester, killed the three children of the household he was lodging in, in Worcester, and left their bodies impaled on railings. The talk, with its accompanying slides, did not go down well. Despite this setback, we held more events, and at the end of that year, we were awarded "Best New Chamber in the World".

One of our early events was a visit to the Worcester Source premises. The Worcester Source was a local newspaper which, at that time, had the distinction of being the oldest continuously produced newspaper in the World. Sadly, I've tried to look it up now, but it seems to be defunct. We were surprised by how many times the printing process required the print to be reversed; we all thought it remarkable that it ever ended up the right way round. One interesting aspect of the visit was a corridor with framed archive copies of newspapers. There was no photography, only beautiful artist-drawn illustrations of, for example, the Boer War. We were even more fascinated that the price on one copy was 4d, at a time when that would have been an incredible amount of money. We were told that the government of the day taxed it deliberately to make it too expensive for ordinary people to afford because they did not want them to know too much of what was going on. What a contrast to today's mass information distribution systems.

Some years later, in 1986, when the print workers went on strike in Wapping, I was not surprised. The cause of the dispute was the attempt by Rupert Murdoch to introduce new computerised methods, by which the content could be input directly, without the need for the "hot-metal linotype", thus rendering the print workers redundant. What we had seen at the Source was so convoluted a process that I could see why there should be a desire to simplify it.

We did some events for charity, including a "bed push" around Worcester. A team of us was pushing while others took collecting tins for the onlookers. At one point, we paused, and my team were slightly intimidated at the sight of a group of "goths" dressed all in black, complete with chains, huge boots and rings through their noses – until one girl detached herself, bounced over to us and said, 'Hi, Mrs B, they'll all give you some money.' I was her form teacher!

I mentioned the computer room in Plessey in the 1970s, but it was 1981 that the personal computer was introduced with the launch of the Acorn Electron. I concede that I did not at first see the significance of a personal computer. It just seemed like a vehicle for playing games or a sophisticated typewriter. I had no idea how ubiquitous computer technology would become. Mobile phones were becoming available. They had actually been invented in about 1973, but there is always a long lead time between an innovation and its commercial availability. The first models were bulky, confined to car 'phones, and restricted by available networks. My husband had insisted on having an early model in his car.

The question arose of which chamber would host the Regional Conference. Because we were at the extremity of the region, there was some scepticism as to whether the majority of the region's members would attend a regional conference in Worcester, so we made a comprehensive marketing effort, going round all the Chambers in the region with our state-of-the-art presentation – a slide tape presentation; no PowerPoint then – and the event was a great success.

Coventry, the largest Chamber in the region hosted the World Congress. We persuaded the Lee and Perrins factory to give us 600 small presentation bottles of Worcestershire Sauce with labels "With the compliments of Worcester Junior Chamber – Best new chamber in the World." A few of us held a "labelling party" to stick all the labels on the bottles.

War touched us in 1982 with the Falklands conflict. The Falkland Islands were a group of islands off Argentina but a British Overseas Territory. Argentina had long disputed the sovereignty of the islands, and President Galtieri decided to invade and claim them. Most of the islanders were of British descent and did not want to be under Argentine control. The British foreign secretary, Lord Carrington, was taken by surprise by the invasion and resigned. My French pen friend Suzanne's teenage daughter Isabelle was staying with us at the time to improve her English and insisted I explain what was going on. I tried to explain that he had made a mistake and felt the only honourable thing to do was to resign, but it was clear she did not understand. It dawned on me that she understood the words, but not the concept, because in French politics, it would not have been necessary to resign. I finally knew I had succeeded in my explanation when she said, '*Ah*, like the Japanese committing suicide!' I said, 'Yes, but in Britain, it is not necessary to fall on your sword, only to resign.'

In the weeks that followed the invasion, many restrictions were placed on the islanders. Some were deported, and others were imprisoned. The British government, under Margaret Thatcher, decided to resist the invasion and launched a task force of all three branches of the services: Army, Airforce and Navy to retake the islands. The United Nations condemned the Argentine invasion and supported Britain. The conflict lasted seventy-four days and cost 900 lives before the Argentinians surrendered and the territory returned to British control.

There were two other notable events for Worcester Junior Chamber. The National President would host a President's day – a sort of "Jeux sans Frontiers", with fun team games – which we decided to attend. I persuaded everyone that we needed to get fit, not with any expectation of winning anything, but just so that we could enjoy the day without being exhausted. We met twice a week at the Racecourse to train, but then rather spoiled it by going for a drink! The second event was a Charity Raft Race. Competitors had to construct the raft and race it. We put together a team of ladies and called ourselves "The Worcester Chamber Maids". Unfortunately, the race was cancelled on the day because there had been a lot of rain and the river was in flood, but we'd had fun making the raft and our costumes.

1982 was also the year in which the "Mary Rose" was finally raised. She was a flagship of Henry VIII's Navy and had been sunk in 1545. She had been located in 1971, but it was felt that technology was not sufficiently advanced to raise her successfully. It was one of the most costly and complex maritime salvage operations of all time, but the ship herself and the vast collection of artefacts present a time capsule of Tudor life and conditions.

In the year after being president, it is customary in Junior Chamber to be designated IPP – Immediate past president, whose job it is to support and advise the new president – a sort of backstop. I enjoyed the role with the new president, Nick. I told him, 'When you need something and have tried everyone else, ask me and the answer will be "yes".' He needed to do it only once during his presidency.

I was elected Chairman of the Regional Group and enjoyed going to National Council meetings and the National Conferences.

The heir to the throne, Prince William was born.

The Cold War was continuing with strained relationships with the USSR. In 1983, a Korean flight mistakenly flew into USSR airspace and was shot down, killing all 269 people on board. The USSR's suspicious attitude dated back to the Korean War of 1950, when yet another proxy war occurred. Communist North Vietnam, backed by the USSR and China, invaded South Korea, which was backed by the USA. The war ended in 1953 after more than 1million combat casualties. As in other examples, it appears that the root of the problems was the partition of different factions after WWII.

Chapter 15
Move to Britannia Square

John was discontented with our house and wanted something grander, so we moved to a Grade 2 listed building in Britannia Square, one of the best-preserved Georgian squares in the country. It was three storeys and a basement, and the rooms had twelve-feet-high ceilings. The centre of the square was a pleasant green space occupied by the Junior department of the Alice Ottley School. Although it was a grand house, it did have some faults: the front door did not close properly, and the sash windows in the bedrooms could not be pulled right down. One night, I was alone in the house with the boys when I was awakened by a loud bang. I was afraid there was someone in the house, but I had to investigate, because of the boys. The wind was howling through the front door, but I made myself go down into the basement – nothing – I emerged again and started back up the stairs. I looked up in trepidation and to my surprise saw that the trapdoor, which was way above the staircase and led to the roof space, had been lifted up and dropped back down to one side. It was obvious that no one could have reached it without a ladder, and even that would have been very precarious. It dawned on me that a gust of wind must have blown straight up the three flights of the staircase and been strong enough to lift the wooden door.

I learned later that John was having another affair at this time, which upset me as I felt he should not have put us through the disruption of moving, knowing his situation. After a while, he again said he wanted a divorce. At that time, the divorce laws were different from today. He did not have grounds for divorce, only I did, because of his adultery, so I had to be the one to sue for divorce, even though it was he who wanted it. There was not much point in my refusing to sue for divorce when he was living with someone else and using our joint bank account.

We would obviously have to sell the house, but because we had had a damp-proof course installed, all the walls had been stripped up to a height of two feet, so every downstairs room needed to be redecorated. He said he would come to help, but somehow other things always got in the way, and he never did. He procrastinated over the divorce for quite a long time. I later realised that he thought it would look better on his CV for the divorce to be on the grounds of two years of separation rather than his adultery.

In 1984, Pop star Bob Geldof saw a programme about the famine in Ethiopia and decided to put all his contacts in the music business to use to do something about it. He and Midge Ure formed Band Aid, a rock band and charity. Their song "Do They Know it's Christmas?" was a no.1 hit and raised millions for the charity. A Band Aid concert, at which Bob enlisted top artists, raised similar sums, and in subsequent years, "Live Aid" and further reincarnations of Band Aid continued the good work.

In contrast, 1984 also saw another dispute in the mining industry with the year-long strike led by Arthur Scargill. Many observers called the strike "the most bitter industrial dispute in British history". The miners' strategy was similar to that employed in 1972: to cause disruption by creating an energy crisis, but Prime Minister Margaret Thatcher had caused coal to be stockpiled and used police to stop the flying pickets from preventing non-striking miners from working. The strike was declared illegal because no national ballot of members had been held. The defeat of the NUM significantly weakened the Trade Union movement. The much-reduced coal industry was privatised at the end of 1984.

By now, I was teaching full-time at the Alice Ottley School. Tim was at King's School, and Steve was due to go there the next term. John said he could not afford to pay school fees (despite being a managing director.) Because I thought the boys had been through enough upheaval without changing schools and being separated from their friends, I went to see the headmistress. It was usual for teachers in schools such as Alice Ottley and King's to receive a reduction in fees, but obviously, it was of no benefit to a teacher at Alice Ottley with boys or a teacher at King's with girls, unless reciprocal arrangements could be agreed. She said she would try again to get the arrangements in place, but unfortunately, it was not possible. A part-time post came up at King's, so I applied. I was offered the job but was warned that while I was the best candidate for a part-time post, that would not necessarily be the case if it became a full-time post, because the field of candidates would be much wider and include men and people who were prepared to relocate. I appreciated the candidness of the warning, but decided to risk it anyway – even though it would mean a drop in salary, to get the fee reduction. When I told John, expecting him to say he would make up the drop in salary, because the overall figure was less, he said, 'Oh, no, you're not saving me money you're costing me money – I wasn't going to pay the fees at all.' I took the post, and shortly afterwards found another part-time post in a rather strange little boarding school called "St Cloud". It catered largely for foreign students and boys who had not fared well at other schools. There were some students from cultures which did not respect women, so teaching maths to students who did not consider women significant and were not prepared to admit to a woman that they did not understand was very difficult. Fortunately, at the end of the term, I was offered a full-time post at King's. At the time, it was an all-boys school except for the sixth form, which accepted girls. I was one of only four women on the staff.

The world was shocked by the worst industrial accident in history up until then, in Bhopal in India. Dangerous methyl isocyanate gas leaked from an insecticide plant owned by an Indian subsidiary of the American Union Carbide Corporation, killing thousands immediately and causing suffering for years. It is estimated that 15,000 to 20,000 died, and half a million survivors were affected with a range of problems such as respiratory disease and blindness. Almost as shocking as the leak itself, was the fact that very little compensation was awarded to survivors, and even though it was shown to be due to poor procedures and safety systems, neither Dow Chemicals, which bought out Union Carbide, nor the Indian government were brought to account or made to decontaminate the site properly. The only repercussions were not until 2010, when some former executives, all Indian citizens, were convicted of negligence.

By then, my boys were pressing for a personal computer in the shape of a Sinclair ZX Spectrum, and I conceded on the basis that developing keyboard skills might be useful to them in the future. I had no idea how ubiquitous computer technology would become. I remember a game called "Rubble Trouble", in which your icon chased little creatures through a maze, trying to zap them. However, the walls of the maze could dissolve, exposing your icon to be zapped back by the monsters. I did once try to write a programme, but it was very tedious, and a tiny mistake somewhere in the mass of lines was very difficult to find. Hats off to Ada Lovelace, the daughter of Lord Byron, who wrote the first computer programme back in 1848. Charles and Diana's second son, Prince Harry was born.

The history of DNA (Deoxyribonucleic acid) is another example of the "slow burn" from its first discovery to an entity with which everyone is familiar. A lot of people will associate the discovery of the "double helix" of the DNA molecule with James Watson and Francis Crick around 1953. In fact, credit should also have been given to Rosalind Franklin. Could it have been the fact that she was a woman that caused her to have been overlooked for a Nobel Prize? All the researchers, in fact, relied heavily on previous research, and original ideas on the topic go back long before this generation. Nowadays DNA is ubiquitous in applications such as discovering ancestry, paternity, tracing heritage, investigating the origins of populations and perhaps most visibly in identifying criminals very accurately from the most minute traces of blood, skin or hair. It was not until 1985 that its use in forensics was proposed, and it was first used in the case of the death of sixteen-year-old Dawn Ashworth in 1986. Tests were done in that case and another one from a few years earlier, which showed that the same killer was responsible for the two deaths, but it was not the suspect that the police had. They organised a mass DNA testing of males, without result. It was not until Colin Pitchfork was overheard boasting that he had bribed someone to take the test for him that police got their man, and he was convicted of murder. He served thirty-three years in prison. Nowadays, DNA is one of the main tools of forensic investigation, and many cold cases, which were unsolvable before its introduction, are being revisited.

Chapter 16
Building a New life

I moved to a three bedroom semi in Morrin Close on the outskirts of Worcester. The divorce laws of the time basically dictated that, because I was well qualified, I should earn my own living and was not entitled to maintenance for myself, even though I had sacrificed my career to John's and stopped work to look after the boys while they were young. I was left with just £4000 for a deposit on the house, and in a time of soaring inflation, I had to take a large mortgage. The maintenance I got for the boys did not even cover that mortgage. I think I could have got over John more easily if I hadn't had to see him again, but because of the boys, I had to make the effort. It was important that they maintain a relationship with him, even though it was me who had to do all the arranging and driving to make it happen.

The neighbours must have thought I was crazy; the day I moved in, I dug up the front lawn! There was a good explanation, though. I had ordered some bulbs and other plants, which were to be delivered at the best time for planting, and that turned out to be that day. I had to cut away some of the lawn to make space for the plants. I settled on leaving a central oval of lawn (the maths came in handy, working out how to do that) with corner areas for the plants.

I discovered that the central heating did not work, and I needed a new boiler. I can remember the three of us sitting on the settee wrapped in three quilts – so cold that no one wanted to get up to make a cup of tea. I could not afford the full price of the boiler so negotiated a staged payment scheme. I was surprised and intimidated a few months later to receive a court summons to which I was supposed to reply, but the boxes did not offer a way of explaining the situation. It just asked, 'Do you dispute that you owe the money?' Well, yes, I did owe the money, but I was not in arrears because of the staged payment scheme. I was really panicking, having never had a court order before. My friend Ginny, a solicitor, was due to come round. She and I, and our four children, were going to her mother's cottage in Minehead for a week's holiday. She took one look at it and said, 'No problem, I'll sort it.' I was so relieved.

The head of physics at King's eased me in gently. For the first year, I did not have the responsibility of a final year GCSE or A-level class and had two of each of the other classes per week, so I quickly got used to the syllabus. I was delighted to be teaching the Nuffield syllabus again. I did find a big difference in teaching boys as opposed to girls. If the girls liked you, they would respond, but with the boys, you had to establish who was boss, and there was always a tendency towards mischief. The syllabus required the topic of waves to be taught using "Ripple Tanks", and in those days, much of the apparatus was homemade, rather than commercially bought. Ours consisted of a window frame with screw-in rods as legs, which were perfect as a make-believe sword. If you took your eyes off the boys, they would be mock sword fighting and, of course, water and boys are a recipe for disaster. Nowadays, most schools are mixed. The next year, I took the classes during their examination year.

BMX bikes were the craze, so I built a quarter-pipe for the boys, which they used in front of the garage. However, it attracted all the youngsters in the area. The neighbours complained about the noise, with justification. The boys took the quarter-pipe to the local recreation ground and used it there. To my surprise, it was never misused and always returned at the end of the day.

A friend of Steve's at school had a garter snake as a pet, so Steve wanted one too. Finally, reluctantly. I agreed. It was very pretty and lived in a glass tank. Steve fed it whitebait. It was no trouble until one day, the top of the tank must have been slightly open because the snake escaped. Margaret, a lovely lady who came in a couple of times a week to help, was terrified when she was told it was loose, but she did not come across it, and Steve found it when he came home.

Most people will remember the Chernobyl disaster. During a test at the nuclear power plant in Pripyat, Ukraine, then part of the USSR, there was an explosion and subsequent fire that destroyed the containment building and released radioactive material. The test should have been carried out during the day shift, with employees well informed and prepared, but for various reasons, it was delayed, and there was far less time to ensure everyone was informed and prepared. At first, it was not acknowledged by the USSR, and it was a power station in Sweden which first noticed unusual levels of radiation. The USSR initially denied there had been an accident, then reported only a minor one, but finally issued a statement – a masterpiece in understatement! *"There has been an accident at the Chernobyl Nuclear Power Plant. One of the nuclear reactors has been damaged. The effects of the accident are being remedied. Assistance has been provided for any affected people. An investigation commission has been set up."*

Since the Soviet authorities were so reluctant to provide information, it is difficult to have figures, but certainly, a vast area was evacuated, a number of people died, and many people suffered ARS (Acute Radiation Syndrome) leading to long-term problems for years afterwards. The radiation spread all over Europe, but in varying degrees of severity, depending on factors such as weather patterns. Mountainous areas like the Alps and Welsh and Scottish Highlands were particularly badly affected. Many European countries banned the import of certain foods. Some of those restrictions were not lifted until 2012. Trends of mutation and lack of fertility were noted in flora and fauna for many years. It reminded me of John Wyndham's *The Chrysalids*, set in a post-nuclear environment, which I had read as a teenager. Even though British reactors were of a different design, which would not have behaved in the same way and British safety procedures were better, the population developed a deep distrust of nuclear power.

Up until my divorce, our standard of living had depended largely on my husband's salary, with any income from me as a bonus. However, I now realised that it would depend on my income alone, and who knew what the future held. Even though I had a stable post at King's, I wanted to have the freedom to move if circumstances dictated, and I recognised that things were changing rapidly, with the increasing input of computer technology. So, I decided I should take some courses to stay up to date. I investigated at the local library and came across the Open University. I decided that if I was going to study, I might as well do it properly, so I signed up for a degree course, that would begin in February of the next year. There was information about help with fees, and when I sent in the figures of my income and expenditure, it transpired that they would reduce the fees to just £50 which was a great help.

It was necessary to do a foundation course. Obviously, they

would not let me do a foundation course in maths or science, and I did not see the relevance of one in arts subjects, so I took the "Living with Technology" option. It was excellent and really helped to keep abreast of advances in technology. One topic dealt with the problem of fossil fuels running out. It discussed the options and gave all the facts and figures. It became obvious that although alternatives such as solar energy, wind turbines, wave machines, biomass, etc were helpful, they could never be enough to provide all the world's energy needs. I concluded that the only long-term solution is nuclear fusion; unfortunately, it is not yet possible. I remain convinced that this is the only solution for the world and that all other options are useful in buying time until we can achieve energy production by nuclear fusion. Of course, there is still the problem of people's perception of nuclear energy, which is not helped by the fact that the media do not differentiate between nuclear fission and nuclear fusion. Nuclear fusion is the process that occurs in the sun. It is completely different from the fission process, which drives all current nuclear power plants. It does not produce any harmful waste, and there is no problem with radiation. In those days, research was in its infancy, and even today, when small-scale reactions have been achieved, it is still a long way from a commercially viable option. There were problems in the development of the other options, too. With wind and wave power, for example, the difficulty is that a large amount of wind or wave force is necessary to make the devices work, but that same amount of force makes them liable to structural failure.

One of the topics on the GCSE syllabus was energy options, and the material I had studied on the course was very helpful. There was a summer school for a week at Bristol University. I really enjoyed the activities, which included writing a computer programme to control the timings of a washing machine, calculating the stresses and strains in a roof truss and making a model, doing calculations on the economics of a chemical process, and methods of analysing the water quality of a stream. This last one I was able to use directly at King's. In a conversation with the head of geography, he outlined the field trip he was planning for his A-level students, which would contribute to their coursework. It transpired he wanted to do just the sort of investigation I had learned. I went on the trip and ran that section of the work.

I badly needed a new carpet for the lounge but did not have any capital available, so I decided to apply to mark for the Cambridge exams. I was accepted to mark an external GCSE exam for pupils in Zimbabwe. There was one question for sixteen marks, which simply asked them to describe the workings of the internal combustion engine. It was quite difficult to mark since their English was not very good, so I had to try to decipher what they were trying to say and see if there was anything I could award marks for. Nowadays, questions are much more structured, so the science knowledge is not quite so dependent on a pupil's ability to express it in language.

The latest home entertainment was videos, more often rented than bought. The system acted like a library: you joined, and then had access to a catalogue of titles which could be rented for a few days for a fee. The boys pestered for a video recorder. I investigated the market and found there were two systems: VHS and Betamax. Betamax was the best system, technically, so I opted for that. Unfortunately, we had just entered the era where marketing was becoming more significant than quality in successful selling. VHS was mass marketed, which meant that videos were mainly made in VHS format, not Betamax, and consequently, it was hard to get popular videos in Betamax. I had to capitulate and buy a VHS. I feel that today's situation is even more extreme in terms of the dominance of marketing.

CDs (Compact discs) had actually been invented in 1982 in Japan, but by now, they were beginning to have an impact on the music market. Later, their use would be extended to non-audio as CD-ROM (Read-Only-Memory) for computer input. By 2007, 200 billion CDs had been sold. I was reminded of one of my boyfriends at Oxford in the late '60s, who had his state-of-the-art record player carefully delivered to his room. The reproduction was amazing, but of course, that meant it would reproduce any tiny imperfection as well. It took him about ten minutes cleaning and prepping to put a record on!

Making my own life did not just involve my working life. I realised that I was now responsible for the maintenance of the house and the car, and I was conscious that failure to keep on top of things would result in problems and extra cost. So, I set about knowing how to do such things as inspect for any problems with the roof and keep the gutters clear.

My pen friend Suzanne came over to see me again. She wanted a present to take back for her mother, who, rather unusually for a French woman, did not drink coffee—only tea. So, what better present than a Worcester porcelain teapot? My only concern was how to pack and post it. I need not have worried; at the till they said, 'Oh, don't worry. We take care of all that, just give us the address, and if it doesn't arrive or is broken, we'll keep sending another one until it is successful.' We were very impressed.

There were a couple of winters when it snowed quite a lot – it was a pain if it was during the week, but lovely if it was on Sunday. I remember one occasion when the boys and I took their sledge to the Malvern Hills. The sled was a magnificent affair with side runners, a seat, and a separate front runner with a steering wheel. It was the envy of everyone on the slopes, but the boys were very generous in letting other people have a go. As I drove away, the roads were very icy, and at the bottom of the hill, we saw a car had mounted the curb and run into the garden of a house. I got out to see if anyone needed help, to be told by the lady of the house. 'Yes, thanks, it's OK. This is the third time this winter!'

For the second module of my OU degree, I took "Modelling with Maths". I intended to do the electronics module, and the maths module was recommended as a prerequisite. I knew my maths was probably already good enough, but I thought that revision would do me no harm. I thoroughly enjoyed it. The problems were all set in real-world situations. The summer school was at Warwick University, and one evening, I had a surreal experience. Walking back to my room, I passed a culvert with sloping grassy banks. I had had a drink or two, but not enough to give me hallucinations, yet the whole bank seemed to be moving. When I looked more closely, I saw that the entire bank was, in fact, a mass of frogs.

When I had attended Tim's first parents' evening at King's, his teachers had been somewhat critical of his progress. I said, 'I'm just surprised you've managed to keep him still enough to teach him anything.' At the Christmas concert, Tim did not take a significant part, because, like me, singing is not his forte, but he did sit perfectly still and stood up and sat down in all the right places – progress! By 1986, he was in the senior part of the school and was part of a rugby team which was unbeaten for the whole season. I ran an after-school gym club in which both Tim and Steve took part. In the display, Steve drew a huge gasp from the audience with his vault over the long box. He took off, did not touch the box at all, scored high over it with a straight body, and dropped into a forward roll at the end.

I had never taken to acting. At the high school, when we were in the sixth form we were encouraged to broaden our interests for the sake of university applications, so I did get involved in the school play, but not as an actress. I was in charge of the lighting. The production was Shakespeare's *The Tempest*, which required some rather dramatic effects, particularly the stormy shipwreck scene. It was all manual responding to verbal or visual cues – no computer programmed sequence. We had only three banks of lights and three dimmers, so it was a complicated sequence of plugging and unplugging, along with synchronised sliding up and down for me and my colleague Ann. The whole cast, who were not actually on stage, used to come and watch, and we warned the teacher who was acting as producer that if the scene overran by a few seconds, the whole lot was likely to overheat and burn out.

When a notice went up at King's for the staff panto, which was apparently performed biennially, I volunteered to help backstage. However, someone put a huge arrow across to the acting column, so I found myself on stage. I actually enjoyed it, though I do not think I contributed very much to the musical aspect of it.

Sometime after that, I was asked to do the choreography for the school production of *Cabaret*. Although I loved dancing, I had never done anything like that, but I enjoyed it. I had a lovely group of girls to work with, who could all do the splits, so I had lots of scope; however, the boys all had two left feet. I gave up on using a dance involving the boys in the "KIT KAT Club" scene and decided instead that the girls would do a cancan, which was appropriate because, although the club was set in Germany, the cancan was the rage all over Europe at the time the story was set. I made red circular tablecloths, lined with black lace frills, done up with Velcro, so the girls just whipped the cloths off the tables, wrapped them around their waists, and danced the cancan complete with high kicks and the splits. One of the A-level physics students had decided that for his coursework project, he would design a computer-controlled electronic circuit, which then translated to macroscale with normal lights to produce a sequence of lights for the "CABARET" sign above the KitKat club. It moved through each letter, illuminating one after the other, then to the whole sign flashing on and off a few times to a brief blackout before beginning all over again. It was very effective.

Chapter 17
Stable Life

In 1987, I fell ill with flu-like symptoms. I went to the doctor, but he just sent me home with paracetamol. I deteriorated. One night, I was so bad that the boys called my friend Lesley, who called the doctor. He again just said, 'Flu, but I suppose I'd better take a blood test.' He looked at the oscilloscope sitting on the table, which was there because I was doing the electronics course at the OU, and asked what I did for a living. I told him I taught his son – I had never seen him at a parents' evening! A couple of days later, I had a call from the surgery, which said that they were very sorry; the tests showed I had had pneumonia and a massive bacterial infection! I had fought it off with just paracetamol. For the first time in my life, I had been physically incapable of smoking. When I started smoking, there was no real evidence that it was harmful, and the idea that passive smoking could be dangerous seemed ridiculous. I like to think that if I had known how dangerous it is, I would not have started, but who knows? By the time I was pregnant, more evidence had been gathered, but it was still not conclusive; nonetheless, I felt that whereas I could make decisions about my own health, if there was any suggestion of danger to my unborn child, I did not have the right to take the risk. In each case, I started again as soon as I had given birth. I had also tried to give up once before when John had implied that it was one of the reasons for the state of our relationship, but he said, 'Oh, for goodness sake, start smoking again, you're like a bear with a sore head', so I did not have much motivation or support. This time, since I had not had a cigarette for nearly two weeks, I thought I would be crazy not to try, even though I had a pack of 200 in the cupboard. I was doing all right until one day when the boys were playing up. I got so close to having one.

I rang my friend Val, and she said, 'Don't. Just hang on until I get there. I'll be there in ten minutes.' She stayed with me for four hours. If she had not done that, I think I would still be smoking to this day. These days, it is common knowledge how harmful smoking is, but campaigns to persuade people to stop, or better still, youngsters not to start, seem to be backfiring. Vapes, introduced as a less harmful alternative to help people stop smoking, are instead being used by youngsters who have never smoked before. There are suggestions that the marketing is at fault for targeting youngsters with colours and flavours.

Because King's is a boarding school, there were lessons on Saturday mornings, and staff who did not live in school were encouraged to help the house staff with Sunday activities. I ran an activity which I had come across in the Junior Chamber called "The World Trade Game". It involved each pair of players acting as a country and being given realistic tokens of the goods they had to trade. It was played in one-year periods. At the end of each year's trading, it was all added up and reset, so it was a bit hectic at the end of each period but otherwise was great fun and educational. In those days, the tokens were all wooden, and everything was manual. It was stored in a huge box. Nowadays, I've no doubt it has been computerized.

The fact that I had done the OU electronics course was a boon, but the ISMEC (Independent Schools Micro-Electronics Course) which I had to teach, was so well structured, it was easy.

The boys did a series of guided experiments with modular equipment, drew conclusions and studied how the systems worked. On the OU course, we had studied how to change an analogue signal to a digital one and back again. It could be said that single development was the foundation of our whole, modern digital age. The properties of digital signals had been known for a long time, but until then, the process of changing from an analogue signal had just been too complex.

I remember being shocked by two events that year: The Enniskillen bombings by the IRA (Irish Republican Army) at a Remembrance Day service saw the deaths of twelve people, and the King's Cross fire killed thirty-one and injured a hundred. The fire was believed to have been started when a lit match was dropped onto rubbish accumulating under an escalator. It had not appeared too serious until a flashover into the booking hall. The fire led to a ban on smoking at all stations.

The boys had access to a sub-aqua club run by professional leaders from the local club, but they needed a staff liaison; since Tim was keen to join the club, he persuaded me to act as liaison. Every Monday lunchtime, the boys helped me take the tanks to the club to be filled up. After school on Mondays, we would be in the pool. I enjoyed it, but the chlorine in the water made my hair very dry and flaky, even though I stood under the shower with conditioner for ages.

King's had a resource called "The Old Chapel" in Wales. It really was an old chapel, adapted for adventure holidays. The junior school used it, and the entire middle school used to go there a class at a time for a week, and of course, the CCF (Combined Cadet Force) used it as well. The CCF is an organisation sponsored by the Ministry of Defence which operates in schools. Its aims are to develop leadership skills and encourage self-reliance, endurance, and responsibility. On Wednesday afternoons, I taught the boys first aid. There were four girls in the sixth form who wanted to go on the training week for the cadets at the Old Chapel, so they needed a female member of staff. We canoed about 10 miles the first day and also did caving. The concept of absolute darkness was brought home to me when we were all told to switch off our forehead lights. It was a very intimidating experience. Most of the food consisted of rations supplied by the army, but I was very impressed with the boys' system for making the packed lunches: a production line, where the first boy slapped butter on the slices of bread, the next put the corned beef on, the next applied the pickle, and the last one wrapped the sandwich in tinfoil – very efficient.

The population was aghast when Terry Waite, a special envoy for the Archbishop of Canterbury, was kidnapped in Beirut, having travelled to Lebanon to try to secure the release of four previously kidnapped hostages. He agreed to meet the captors to negotiate, but instead they kidnapped him. He was held in solitary confinement for four years and not finally released until 1991.

I got involved with the canoe club. Both Tim and Steve joined, but later it was Steve who was to take canoeing seriously. Tim was more interested in rowing. I was chatting with a colleague at the badminton club after school one day when he was bemoaning the fact that he might have to restrict the number of boys on a trip he intended to take to the Lake District for the fourth forms because he was short of one member of staff. I'm not sure how it came about that I volunteered to go, and to take charge of the catering. We were in a hostel-type building. There was still snow on the ground even though it was the Easter holiday. The first day was canoeing. I think I actually started to suffer from exposure. I could not feel my hands at all and was chilled to the bone. Driving back to the hostel, I had to take a very acute left turn, which would not be possible with the canoe trailer on the back, so I decided to drive on, turn around, and then approach from the opposite side, which would make the turn a gentle right turn instead of the acute left. I ended up in a housing estate – the only problem was that I could not find anywhere to turn round and had to say, 'Sorry, boys, I can't get round, the only way is to unhitch the trailer, turn round, then rehitch.' They were as tired as I was, but they were very good, and I did not hear any mention of women's driving.

A couple of days after returning from the Lake District, I was due to go on the Ski trip. I was not a very experienced skier, having been just a couple of times when I was married, but that made me quite valuable as a member of staff because, obviously, the good skiers wanted to be with the more advanced groups, and someone was needed to spend most of the week plodding about picking up the beginners. We went by coach to Austria; it was noisy, but otherwise OK. An advantage was that I could take Tim and Steve for half price. Skiing was later to become a very large part of Tim's life. After we returned, I used to take Tim and Steve as often as I could afford to the Gloucester artificial ski slope. Sadly, it has now closed down.

Michael Ryan hit the headlines in 1987 with the "Hungerford massacre". He shot sixteen people dead, including an unarmed policeman and his own mother, and wounded fifteen others, before killing himself. No motive has ever been established. The attacks were carried out with legally owned weapons. Unlike in the USA where almost every atrocity, although initially met with outrage, fails to result in a change in legislation, a consequence of this event was The Firearms

(Amendment) Act 1988, which limited the use of shotguns with more than 3 cartridges and banned the ownership of semi-automatic rifles. Hungerford is a very pretty town. I was recently at an event in a lovely hotel there; it seems such a shame that it will be forever associated with such sad memories.

I had been on my own for some time by then. I had a few good friends, there were activities associated with school, such as school plays and concerts, and Worcester had a pleasant theatre and a music school connected to the cathedral. I remember two events in particular. There was a play about Edith Piaf. The leading lady was fantastic. I could not believe how well she sang "Non, je ne regrette rien". There was a concert by a visiting Welsh Male Voice choir. I have always loved the richness of the Welsh male voice sound; it seems to wrap around you. I was moved to tears.

Despite having a busy life with a full-time job, bringing up the boys and having these activities, I missed not having a partner. Obviously, without the internet, the only dating possibilities were contacts, friends-of-friends, or a dating agency. Since I had not encountered anyone of any interest, I decided to try an agency. It seemed very respectable and reliable, appearing to do security checks on members, so I felt safe. The first step was to fill in a questionnaire listing interests, hobbies, etc. I ticked a lot of boxes because I took the view that almost anything is interesting with the right person. Unfortunately, the way couples were paired was simply if any one of the hobbies matched. I had a date with a man who was obsessed with spotting discrepancies in films, for example, a discontinuity where someone appears in one outfit, then it changes, or a scene containing something which was not invented until a later date. That was all he could talk about! On another occasion, I had been working hard on my OU degree work, which I could only start after the boys went to bed at ten thirty p.m. I was so tired; I could hardly put two words together and kept nearly falling off the high beer barrel which was the seat. He must have thought I was a moron.

Tim had developed an interest in radio-controlled cars and was very good at repairing and servicing them, so much so, that the local shop paid him to do repairs for customers. One day, Tim was in the shop, when a customer started a conversation with him. Later, as Tim was walking home, a car drew up beside him; it was the same man. At first, Tim thought nothing of it, but gradually he realised he was being propositioned. He had given the man his phone number. Tim came home and told me about it. We decided not to do anything unless something else happened, but the next day the man phoned. We called the police. The police were reassuring and said we had done the right thing in calling them so they could collate data, in case a pattern formed. They reassured us that, normally, such people give up if they receive no encouragement; only very occasionally does it escalate into something more serious. It brought it home to me how plausible people can be. Obviously, I had always taught the boys not to talk to strangers, but this man had almost succeeded in removing himself from the "stranger" category. Tim's interest then expanded to radio-controlled aeroplanes. He used to fly them on the playing field, where members of the local club used to meet. Tim was invited to join their meetings, held in a pub, but since he was so young they met with me to reassure me that it was all above board and promise me he would not be allowed to drink alcohol. They used to have quizzes and competitions, such as aeroplane recognition, which Tim often won!

The boys and I had not been on holiday, other than the school ski trips, for about six years, partly because I could not afford it and partly because I did not think it would be very relaxing. When I saw an advertisement in a magazine for a holiday on the Isle of Wight, travelling by coach and ferry, and emphasising all the available activities, I decided that we should go, particularly as the forecast was for good weather. The journey was a nightmare: we travelled from Worcester by coach to Victoria Coach Station, London, then had to change coaches. The station was dirty, smelly and choking with fumes. I was faced with trying to get lunch, while not leaving the boys or leaving the luggage unattended. In the end, Tim went first while Steve and I guarded the luggage, then Steve and I went. The hotel was pleasant, but I had asked for a room adjoining the boys' room, whereas, in fact, I was some distance away. I was a little anxious. Tim was thirteen and Steve eleven. I had opted for the travel deal, involving the coach and ferry, with free travel vouchers on the island, thinking that for once it would be nice not having to drive, but I found having to be on time waiting for buses more stressful than the driving would have been. There were indeed lots of interesting places to visit and activities for the boys to do, and the other holidaymakers in the hotel were very friendly to us. The sun shone the whole time! I am pleased to say that Victoria Coach Station has had a makeover since then.

My father, a lifelong smoker – in the days when no one knew of the dangers – had a lung removed in his 40s and did not enjoy very good health. After Mum died, he found it difficult to live alone. My brother lived quite close and could go to see him frequently, but it was difficult for me, living further away and with two boys to cope with. I would get a 'phone call saying that he was in hospital again. Each time, I never knew whether I would find him feeling better and sitting up in bed, or be told the worst. On one such occasion, I had managed to get the boys to a friend and drove over to Nuneaton. I was on the slip road curving round to the M6, somewhat distracted, when I was aware that the car was sliding towards the outside lane. The road was wet and very greasy. I tried to correct it but lost control of the car. I ended up spinning round, hitting the crash barrier and spinning back to hit it again before turning over onto the car's side. Thankfully, it dropped back the right way up. Amazingly, my only injury was a bruised ankle. I was on the M6 and nothing hit me. A man came to my aid – though he was very careful not to approach too close, so as not to alarm me – and on discovering that I was unharmed said he would phone for the AA. The car sat outside my house for quite a time before the insurers wrote it off and I was able to buy a replacement. Two weeks later, my father died.

My OU course that year was, "Design Processes and Products" which was very interesting and laid the foundations for my teaching design and technology a few years later. One little snippet of information which I found interesting was that when Sony was considering developing its "Walkman" the ubiquitous portable cassette player, they did a customer survey, the results of which showed there would not be a market for such a product; however, the manager decided to overrule the results and go ahead – it might have cost him his job, but of course, it was a stroke of genius because the Walkman was a great success, paving the way for all modern portable devices.

1988 ended with the Lockerbie bombing. Pan Am Flight 103 was destroyed by a terrorist bomb over the Scottish town of Lockerbie, killing all 243 passengers and 16 crew. Wreckage fell on a residential street, killing another eleven people. A total of 270 deaths made it the worst terrorist attack in British history. It took three years of investigation to identify two Libyan nationals as the culprits, but Colonel Gaddafi at first refused to hand them over. Finally, after a long period of UN sanctions against Libya, Gaddafi handed over the two individuals. In 2001, one of them was finally convicted of murder and jailed for life, but later released as he had prostate cancer. He died in 2012.

My final course for the OU degree was "Design and Innovation". This was built on the "Design Processes and Products" course, but the emphasis was on the transition from design to market. As part of the course, we could either do a case study of a chosen product from inception to commercial viability, or we could actually experience the whole process by designing a product. I was not convinced that I could invent anything, but it was made clear that the case study was not as highly regarded and should be considered a last resort. There was a lot of support material, such as techniques to come up with ideas, how to refine the idea, etc., so I decided to give it a go. Since I made a lot of my own clothes, I had an idea for a tool to help space buttons, but one day when I was in the car with Tim and some of his friends, I said, 'Listen, you lot, is there anything about which you have said, there must be a better way of doing this.' Someone said that it needed three hands to adjust the brakes on a bike. I thought about it and realised he was right. I experienced the problem myself when I was maintaining the boys' bikes. "Braketight" was born. I designed a little gadget which would abut the brakes and turn a screw to tighten or release brake cables. I asked the CDT department at school to make a prototype for me. I did a survey questionnaire at the local cycle shops, finding out what people would be prepared to pay for such a tool, and found out how many bikes are sold in the UK per year. At the summer school, we all signed confidentiality agreements and then showed each other our designs. There was one keen cyclist there who said,

'Have you got a prototype?' He looked at it and declared it a winner. I was delighted. Although it was not part of the course, we were advised about taking out patents. I passed the exams and earned a BA. Ironically, I have 3 degrees all involving science and maths topics, and yet they are all called "A" for arts not "Sc" for science. I believe the OU course can now be called BSc.

At King's, it was decided to totally change the structure of the General Studies course for the sixth form. In addition to the weekly lecture for the whole sixth form, there would be a series of six-week courses, around which groups of students would rotate. Each course would be delivered jointly by two members of staff. I was paired with Steve, who taught English and whom I knew from ski trips. We had the freedom to decide what our course would be about. At first, we had no idea what we could jointly deliver, coming from such disparate disciplines of English and physics. I was invigilating an exam, during which you are not allowed to do anything but sit and watch the group or walk around, when an idea occurred to me. I decided that the most useful skill, which is not directly covered by the various school subjects is the ability to communicate. By the end of the exam, I had mapped out most of the course in my head. Steve embraced the idea enthusiastically. We thoroughly enjoyed delivering our "Communications Skills" course, which culminated in each pupil delivering a five-minute talk on a topic of their choice. We not only had some very interesting talks but also got to know the pupils better. Apparently, ours was the most popular of all the courses.

Nowadays we all accept CCTV as a part of life, though it has always raised concerns about balancing public safety with individual rights. I think most people would agree it greatly contributes to security and Law enforcement. Although it had been used as early as 1942 to observe the V2 rocket testing, it was a very different CCTV from that which we know today. The use of video surveillance became more common in the 1970s when it became possible to record the images, rather than having to observe them directly. Outdoor CCTV was first tested in the UK in Bournemouth in 1985, but it was not really until the late 1980s that it became ubiquitous.

World events sometimes move fast, but it is difficult to match the pace and power of change in 1989. Half a million people gathered in a mass protest about the division of East and West Berlin. East German's communist leaders tried to calm things by offering some concessions, making travel and access to West Germany easier. Sections of the wall were breached, and the communist leadership finally conceded. The wall was officially deconstructed the following year; East and West Germany were reunited, and it sparked the beginning of the demise of the USSR.

The 1980s had seen a few political scandals. Jeffrey Archer had been an MP from 1969 to 1974 but did not seek re-election after a financial scandal left him almost bankrupt. He later regained his standing, reinventing himself as a novelist. In 1986, he resigned as deputy chairman of the Conservative party after a newspaper accused him of paying a prostitute. The next year, he won a civil case against the newspaper and was paid substantial damages, but in 1999, it emerged that he had lied in the 1987 case. He served four years for perjury and perverting the course of justice. Quite a roller-coaster of a life.

Cecil Parkinson was an MP who was forced to resign after revelations that his former secretary, Sara Keays was pregnant with his child in 1983. Although Parkinson paid for the child's support, he never met her or had any other contact. Initial support was with Parkinson, but later opinion swayed towards Sara and her difficulties with the child Flora, who had cerebral palsy and Asperger's syndrome. This shift perhaps indicated a general change in attitudes to extramarital sex.

The Hubble Space Telescope was launched into low Earth orbit in 1990. Because it is outside the Earth's distorting atmosphere, it is able to produce high-quality images and has vastly increased our understanding of the Universe; however, all did not go well initially. The team awaited the first images in a state of great anticipation, but was disappointed when the images were blurred. It proved to be a grinding error in the mirror, which was corrected in a service mission in 1993. One of Hubble's most significant contributions is to determine the rate of expansion of the universe, supporting the Big Bang Theory. The Hubble is predicted to last until 2030–2040.

After my father's death, I inherited a sum of money and had hoped to move to a bigger house, but it appeared that I did not have quite enough to buy anything better than I already had, so I decided to investigate having an extension done. I settled on a two-storey extension to make the lounge and kitchen bigger and give Steve a decent-sized bedroom. I checked at the Town Hall and was told that I did not need planning permission, only compliance with building regulations. The work started while I was on a school ski-trip. Imagine my consternation on my return, to discover that the Town Hall had said they had made a mistake in the measurements, and I *did* need planning permission, which meant that the next-door neighbour had received a letter asking if they had any objections, at a time when the walls were already two feet high! The builders were wonderful. They had been round to see the neighbour to explain that it was not my fault, and I had not been trying to subvert their interests. They even offered to take down the scaffolding every night, so as not to obstruct the shared drive. When they finished the job, they presented me with a huge bouquet of roses. I now had the task of redecorating every room in the house, except my bedroom.

Meanwhile, I had been appointed head of general studies. Early in 1990, I went on a course which was to discussed the pros and cons of doing general studies as an examination subject. At King's, it had never been an exam subject, just courses believed to be important to a rounded education. I think I was finally comfortable with my life. I was a little apprehensive as to what life would be like when the boys left home, but I was otherwise content and confident in who I was. Since I had just been appointed, I had resolved not to contribute (unusual for me!), just listen and learn, but by the time the meeting resumed after lunch, I could restrain myself no longer. I said, 'I'm fed up with this. You all talk as if general studies is about civilising science students – science students read books, they go to the cinema and theatre and listen to music, they do sports. It's the arts students who need educating, they know nothing about science.' There was a rather stunned silence. After the meeting, I found myself talking to two teachers from Christ College, Brecon. I thought one of them was chatting me up, but as I was to find out later, it was the other one – Gareth Jones – who was interested. He said later that he heard me speak, looked up across the green baize tables, and that was it. Thirty years later, we were still together. It is the romance every woman should have.

Part 3

Chapter 18
Meeting Gareth

A couple of days later, I had a phone call at school saying that a Mr Gareth Jones, from Brecon, wanted to speak to me. It took me a moment to place the context. He said he would be in Worcester on business on Friday and could we meet for a drink? I had a feeling that meeting Gareth was important – in fact, I had ducked out of a departmental evening out, to agree to see him – but I had been canoeing in the river the day before and taken a ducking. I think I might have had a mild case of Weil's disease, which can be picked up from river water, because I felt terrible. I was too ill to go to meet him, so I rang the pub where we had agreed to meet, to ask the landlady to convince him that he was not being stood up – I was ill. Apparently, she did a great job. The next day, I was due to go to an examiners' meeting in Birmingham. Although I still felt terrible, I had to go, because if I didn't I would not be eligible to do the marking for the July exams and I needed the money. I am sure I must have been a hazard on the roads; I was in a daze. I did not contribute anything to the meeting, which indicates how ill I felt! I got home and went back to bed. I was upset at missing the rendezvous, because I thought that it was one thing to meet up when he was in Worcester anyway, but perhaps he would not go out of his way for another meeting. On Sunday Gareth rang. He was sympathetic at first, but I could hear a change in his attitude when I explained about having to go to the meeting. He obviously felt that if I was that ill, I would not have gone to the meeting. I thought, *How dare he take such a superior attitude; he obviously does not understand what it is like to need the money.* However, he did suggest another meeting and we overcame this little misunderstanding. We met at a pub halfway between Brecon and Worcester and left my car parked there, had a brief lunch and continued in his car, back towards Brecon. The Brecon Beacons National Park is beautiful, and I was admiring the countryside and said, 'Do you like walking?' to which the abrupt answer was 'No', which I thought was a shame and a waste of the beauty, but I did discover that he was a good horseman and liked to enjoy the countryside that way.

It was late afternoon, and I was half expecting Gareth to suggest dinner when he said, 'Would you like a sandwich?' I agreed. It was beautifully presented with garnish. Little did I know that that was the height of his culinary skills and had taken a great deal of effort! We talked until the early hours. I was very tempted to stay the night, but thought it might send the wrong message – in those days, there was more decorum than there is today. He eventually drove me back to my car, but we still could not bear to part; we very nearly drove back to Brecon. When I finally got back home, I rang him and said, 'We have just been very sensible or very silly – I'm not sure which.' A couple of weeks later, we spent the weekend in his caravan in Saundersfoot and from then on met up when we could, either in Brecon or Worcester. It was not easy, since we were both in schools which had Saturday morning lessons and I had the constraints of the boys. He was confident without being arrogant, loving and romantic, and passionate without being aggressive, but the first time we were in Brecon he seemed a different man; insecure and incompetent. I did not know then that he had lost his wife of twenty-seven years just over a year earlier and had been distraught, developed a stutter and had to have time off work. He was at the general studies conference because the school had suggested he become head of general studies, after being head of English for many years. Obviously, his insecurities surfaced when he was at home in Brecon. Gareth's sons were a little perturbed that quite often they could not get an answer from their Dad's phone – no mobiles in those days – so Gareth gave them my number. Whenever I answered the 'phone to Glyn, the eldest son, he would say, 'Is my father there, by any chance?' They must have wondered who this woman was, who had bewitched their father.

Since I had managed to get to the examiners' meeting, I was marking for the Cambridge exam syndicate and, as a team leader, had to go up to Cambridge to do the final checking of papers for a few days. Gareth came with me, and we took the opportunity for me to meet Gareth's three boys, Glyn, Gerwyn and Gethin. I was a bit intimidated, but the evening went well. Gethin was in the army and was about to go back to Berlin for a tour of duty.

The summer holidays were looming, and Gareth asked when he could see me again. I said, 'September, unless you come to Worcester, because I have just had an extension built and the whole house has to be decorated. If it's not finished by the end of the school holidays, it won't get done at all.' I tend to get carried away when I'm working and don't want to stop, but Gareth sensibly insisted that we finish every night at six thirty p.m. We fell into a routine: one night I would cook a meal, one night we would get a takeaway, next night we would have a barbeque (the weather was lovely for most of the time) and the next night we would go out for a meal. Gareth would often whistle as he worked, and I thought, Ah... *how nice. He's content.* He eventually confessed that he hated decorating because he had been made to do it as a boy with his uncle. He was born in 1938 in Swansea, and his father had been killed during the war. His mother would have been in dire straits if it were not for the support of her family, her brothers in particular. Like me, Gareth had passed the 11+ and gone to the grammar school a year early, since Swansea had the same system as Nuneaton had had. I have never met anyone else to whom this applied. As a youngster, when I lived on Greenmoor Road, the Nuneaton Borough football ground was about a mile away down the hill. In the FA Cup, non-league Nuneaton played first division Swansea and the roar when Nuneaton scored could be heard all over the town.

One of my great delights in Gareth was that not only *could* he dance, but he *would* dance. I had a lifelong love of ballroom dancing, but in all my thirteen years married to John, he would never dance with me. He was the managing director of his company, so there were lots of opportunities for functions. He would dance with all the secretaries – It was good for morale, and they all thought he was wonderful – but not with me. The salesmen and regional mangers did not dare to dance with the boss's wife, so I did not get to dance.

One evening, when Gareth and I met in a pub, we each realised the other was excited about something and vied as to who should go first. Sometime earlier, Gareth had written a play called *The Contract of Marriage* and had just heard from his agent that there was a possibility of its being performed at the Old Vic in London. After my OU degree course in Design and Innovation, I had continued to pursue my invention of "Braketight", a device to adjust the tension of bicycle brakes and had just received a letter from Raleigh saying they were interested in it. No wonder we were excited, but sadly, neither of these projects reached fulfilment. I had a patent agent carrying out the searches required for a worldwide patent, but it transpired that someone in the USA had taken out a patent for a very similar device just one month earlier. It meant that although I could manufacture my device in the UK, I could not patent it and so would be vulnerable, and ironically, the better the device was, the more vulnerable I would be to someone undercutting me, so it was not worth pursuing. I still have my prototype. As far as I know, the patent holder has never manufactured it.

In the world outside our bubble, war was looming. Saddam Hussein's Iraq invaded Kuwait. A UN Security Council resolution condemned the invasion, and a coalition of forty-two countries started a build-up of troops in Saudi Arabia, in Operation Desert Shield. Several more resolutions followed, including a demand that Iraq withdraw from Kuwait. Failure to comply led to sanctions against Iraq.

During the summer, King's CCF (Combined Cadet Force) went on a summer camp in Berlin. I had to work very hard to suppress a giggle when my colleagues started to describe and sing the praises of the young regular army officer who had acted as liaison for them – it was Gethin.

When we went back to school in September, we saw each other every weekend, but Gareth said he could not bear to wait that long, so he came to Worcester on Wednesday evenings as well. Each Wednesday on the way home from school I would think to myself, *Gareth won't have eaten; I'll just get a few things in.* The evening would always turn into a romantic candlelit three-course meal for two. After that, Gareth decided he would come over on Tuesdays and Thursdays, instead of just Wednesdays. I had not made our relationship common knowledge because schools can be terrible places for gossip, but our lab technician, Val, was a friend. After I had a wonderful weekend in London, she was all ears for details, but I was speechless – I simply could not find words to do justice to the feelings.

Convinced that we were meant to be together, we used to speculate how we would have met if it had not been for the general studies conference. We settled for my being on the touchline at King's watching Tim play rugby while Gareth was there as the coach of one of the other teams. At that time, he was coaching an also-ran team, which was delighted to be christened "The Iron Dogs". Gareth went down on one knee in front of Worcester Cathedral to propose. We discussed getting married early in the New Year but decided that since Gareth's niece (daughter of his first wife, Helen's, brother), was getting married in February; it would be more diplomatic not to announce our engagement immediately and to plan the wedding for a little later in the year.

I was already committed to the school ski trip again, and Gareth had booked a week's holiday in Morocco. They have about seven days of rain a year, and Gareth was there for four of them! On the coach going to Austria, I opened my book to a lovely surprise; on pages at various intervals were delightful little loving notes from Gareth, just to remind me he was thinking of me. I arrived back in Worcester on the Sunday, and though we had agreed Gareth would come to my house for Christmas on the Tuesday, so that I had time to get the mountain of washing done and do the preparations for Christmas, he 'phoned on Sunday and came straight over. I could hardly see him when he walked in through the clouds of steam from all the washing. We enjoyed a lovely Christmas with Tim and Steve.

As 1991 dawned, Saddam Hussein had still not complied

with the UN resolutions to withdraw from Kuwait, so Operation Desert Storm was launched. During the fighting, Iraq launched missiles at Israel, hoping to prod them into retaliation, which would have brought the Arab world behind Iraq, but Israel was persuaded not to. Despite Saddam Hussein's claim that this would be the "Mother of all battles", the Iraqis were ejected from Kuwait by the end of February. For the following years, there were concerns about Saddam Hussein's "Weapons of Mass Destruction".

Chapter 19
Marriage and Move to Brecon

We set our wedding for 20th July. I decided to use my recently acquired computer skills to typeset the orders of service for the wedding. It was a good job that I was well ahead of schedule, because when I went to collect the finished orders, I noticed the date was incorrect. The printers retrieved my original sheets, and sure enough, the mistake was mine, not theirs! They had to be redone. From then onwards, it became a standing joke that we could never remember whether our anniversary was 20th or 21st July. I had originally said I would have a register office ceremony because I was divorced, but after attending Gareth's niece's church wedding, I felt a church setting added a solemnity to the vows. We were fortunate that King's is the Cathedral school, so as a member of staff, I was eligible for a Service of Blessing in the Cathedral. It was beautiful. The reception was in the Cathedral refectory. I had been making flower displays and ribbon swags for weeks and had friends and family making garlands, so it all looked lovely. Gareth had simply asked me where I wanted to go on a honeymoon and then arranged it all. We spent the first night in Stratford-upon-Avon, and swans even obliged by flying gracefully to land on the river. Next day we spent in Warwick and then drove to Gatwick. We flew to Athens for a few days, taking in the Acropolis. I remember sitting on a rock near the Parthenon and thinking, *Am I really living this; it is like a fairy-tale.* We then joined our ship to cruise around the

Islands before returning to Athens and going down to the Corinth Canal. Gareth christened me his "Princess of Corinth".

Three weeks after our wedding, Gareth's eldest son, Glyn, married his fiancée Nicki, whom he had met at catering college in Birmingham. As he commented in his speech, it had been a busy time; he had acquired a new wife, a new mother and father-in-law, two new sisters-in-law, a new stepmother and two new stepbrothers. The reception was in a marquee in Nicki's parents garden in Kent.

I'm not sure anyone realised just how much the World Wide Web would change our world and way of working. It was invented by Tim Berners-Lee in 1989, while he was working at CERN and was released to the world in 1991. Like all developments, it was a slow burn to reach the ubiquitous state it is today.

Being convinced that the only long-term future for the energy needs of the world is nuclear fusion, I was interested in the progress of the JET (Joint European Torus) project, which had finally resulted in the building of a facility at the UKAEA (United Kingdom Atomic Energy Authority.) in 1983, carrying out research aimed at making nuclear fusion into a viable energy source. Nuclear fusion is the process which takes place in the sun. It necessitates hydrogen atoms colliding at very high speeds. The usual method for trying to achieve the necessary speeds at that time was to have very high temperatures, but the problem was that as soon as the "plasma" of atoms touched the sides of the containment vessel, the heat would be conducted away and the temperature would drop rapidly. At JET, scientists were experimenting with a "Tokamak" – a large doughnut-shaped vessel – which used magnetic containment of the plasma, so that it did not touch the sides. In 1991, for the first time, they used tritium – an isotope of hydrogen consisting of 1 proton and 2 neutrons – as well as deuterium, an isotope with 1 proton and 1 neutron. The JET finally ceased operations in 2023 and is still in the decommissioning process.

During WWII, Lithuania was occupied by the USSR. In 1990, the Republic of Lithuania had been re-established as an independent state and in 1991, the USSR finally recognised Lithuanian independence. This was the first state to leave the USSR and signalled the start of the decline of USSR power and influence, though, as it turned out later, the Russian authorities were not ready to concede totally. Ukraine, the second largest republic after Russia, followed suit towards the end of the year.

I moved to Brecon over the Summer. Tim decided to stay in Worcester and board at King's, while Steve opted to move with me to Brecon and attend Christ College; though he briefly had second thoughts when he realised that, though he was living at home with us, he would have to go back to school after tea and not come home until nine p.m. He was mollified when I pointed out that after tea was homework, which would be easier at school than at home, and recreation where all his friends would be there with him. The received wisdom at the time was that well-qualified physics teachers were very rare, so Christ College must have been one of the few schools in the country which did not need a full-time physicist. There was a time when I did seven part-time jobs: part-time at Christ College; part-time at a little Convent school called St David's, teaching science to pupils aged three plus; part-time at Coleg Powys teaching business studies A-level; teaching first aid to the CCF and as an after school club at St David's; marking for the Cambridge board; writing questions for GNVQ; and doing private tutoring. I kept all my books and resources in the boot of the car because otherwise, I would be sure not to have the right thing in the right place at the right time.

Discussions arose as to arrangements for Christmas. Gareth loved a family Christmas, and I knew that his boys had rallied around to be with their father at Christmas after he lost Helen, but I could feel an undercurrent that they were now facing other commitments to wives/girlfriends and their families, so I suggested we celebrated Christmas in Brecon a week early; I could see the relief in their eyes. I was used to spending a winter holiday in the snow, but to Gareth, a winter holiday meant sun in the Canary Islands, so we went to Tenerife just after Christmas for New Year. Even though I had been told that the weather was good in the Canaries at that time of year, I was still surprised to find myself lying in the sun by the pool.

"Annus horibillis". Although she was not the originator of it, Queen Elizabeth II famously used the phrase to describe her Ruby Jubilee Year of 1992. For several years, the press had been speculating about the state of the relationship between Prince Charles and Princess Diana and following revelations of unfaithfulness on both sides, the pair announced their separation, but at this stage, they were not to divorce, and Diana would still be queen when Charles ascended to the throne. Later, in 1995, following the Bashir TV interview, even the queen agreed that they should divorce, and the marriage was dissolved in 1996. Prince Andrew separated from his wife, Sarah, who was photographed topless with John Bryan. Princess Anne was divorced from her husband, Captain Mark Phillips. There was a fire which almost destroyed Windsor Castle. It was started by a spotlight left too close to a curtain. Builders working in a nearby room attempted to tackle the blaze with fire extinguishers, but it spread quickly. TV pictures showed staff and tradesmen forming human chains to help save precious items, with the queen, in a headscarf, looking distraught. Glyn was driving along the M4 at the time and was horrified to see the flames. The repairs and renovations took five years, and the queen agreed to pay taxes and allow visitors to Buckingham Palace to pay for the bill.

David Mellor, a Cabinet Minister, was forced to resign when his affair with an actress Antonia de Sancha came to light; though, actually, his acceptance of a month's free holiday in Marbella from the daughter of the finance director of the PLO (Palestine Liberation Organisation) was a much more damaging revelation.

Gareth's second son, Gerwyn, married Wendy in Saundersfoot. Glyn and my son Tim got up early and wrote a congratulatory message in huge letters in the sand on the beach outside the hotel. We had decided to stay in the caravan for the second night. It was a rather old van, and it was a good job that my outfit included knee-length boots, because the floor of the bedroom gave way and I found myself with one leg through the floor and the other horizontally. Gareth had to pull me out very carefully since the ends of the floor formed a sort of barb to stop me from getting out.

For the Christmas holiday that year, we had booked to go on a cruise down the Nile, but there were several incidents of terrorists shooting tourists, so the foreign office was advising against visiting. Booking a holiday in those days was very different to how it is today. The process involved collecting a brochure from a travel agent, choosing a holiday and going back to the agent, who would then 'phone up to see if the holiday was available. If it were not, you would start all over again, which was rather tedious. At such short notice, we decided that the process was not really viable, so we just said, 'Tell us what is available.' It turned out to be Majorca; guaranteed a three-star hotel, but not being told which resort. It was Magaluf. Not exactly our first choice, but we had no other option. The weather was not guaranteed at that time of the year, but it was sunny and not too cold most of the time. The pool was closed, but there were some nice trips available. We particularly enjoyed the "Cuevas del Drach", which I had actually visited when on holiday with my parents, years earlier. Exactly as it had been then, the highlight was a candlelit barge coming across the water with a string quartet playing Offenbach's "Barcarole".

The Maastrict Treaty, which had been signed the year before, came into effect in 1993. As the foundation of the EU (European Union), it laid out the details for the increased cooperation between members in finance, commerce and legal matters.

Gareth sang with "Talgarth Male Voice Choir" and of course, I became a "groupie", going to all the concerts – though the best singing was always in the pub afterwards. After a while, I decided that I must learn the Welsh National Anthem because the concerts always ended with a rousing rendition. I can't sing, but at least with everyone in such a good voice, I could make an attempt. The choir also used to go "on tour", which is a euphemism for finding a place and securing an invite to go and sing a couple of concerts and generally have a good time. We had a lovely visit to Brittany. I was astounded to discover that their anthem is to the same tune as the Welsh anthem, and the Welsh speakers and French could understand each other because Breton is so similar to Welsh. Gareth also took part in the 10,000 Voices event in Cardiff Arms Park, with Shirley Bassey singing. I was slightly disappointed because the sheer numbers involved meant the audience was a long way away, so the music was relayed by microphones. To me, it didn't feel like a live performance and being Wales it rained… and rained…

After the end of the Gulf War, there were concerns that Iraq would invade Kuwait again. In 1992, Saddam Hussein refused to abide by a UN Security Council disarmament resolution, this and other concerns had led to the establishment of the "no-fly zone", but Iraq did not respect it and in 1993, amid fears of growing aggression from Iraq, the US, UK and France carried out a number of strikes on mobile missile sites, which had been moved into the no-fly zone.

In the USA, agents of the Bureau of Alcohol, Firearms and Tobacco suspected that members of the cult "The Branch Davidians" led by David Koresh, of storing illegal arms and secured a warrant to search their compound outside Waco in Texas. Unfortunately, a reporter inadvertently tipped off the Davidians, so when the AFT attempted to enforce the warrant, a pitched battle ensued, leading to the deaths of four agents and six Davidians. A siege lasting fifty-one days followed, culminating in a massive fire. Accounts differ as to what exactly happened and who was responsible, but the net result was the deaths of 76 Davidians.

Tim was born on the 21st October 1975, so 1993 was his 18th birthday. He came to Brecon for a celebration dinner. At this point, he was in his A-level year at King's and rowing seriously. He had been part of a number of winning crews, including a coxless pair, who were up for GB selection. He was looking at options for a career in the Armed Forces.

We had a lovely family Christmas in Brecon with Glyn and Nicki, Gethin, Gerwyn and Wendy and Steve, before Gareth and I flew to Lanzarote for some winter sun and relaxation. The camel ride was an experience!

Throughout 1994 there were still problems with Iraq. Saddam Hussein would push everything to the limit. Refusing to cooperate then finally complying just before a deadline. There were still grave concerns about WMD and his intentions towards Kuwait.

Fortunately for the population of an increasingly unstable world, there was some good news in the shape of the Kremlin Accords, in which Boris Yeltsin of the Russian Federation and Bill Clinton of the USA agreed to desist from pointing nuclear weapons at strategic targets in each other's country. A nuclear arsenal in Ukraine was also destroyed.

A moment in history for South Africa occurred when the first multiracial elections were held, and Nelson Mandela was elected.

Everyone will remember the appalling revelations at 25th Cromwell Street in Gloucester. The police had already encountered Fred West, but the cases had always folded before trial. They enacted a search warrant in February 1994 and found a body buried in the garden. A horrified population reeled as further bodies were found and the story gradually emerged of at least twelve murders, between 1967 and 1987 and a catalogue of rape, torture, bondage and mutilation of their daughters and other young women; Fred's second wife, Rose, being complicit in many of them. The whole story from a dysfunctional upbringing to the final cruelty is so far from most people's experience as to seem like fiction. The couple were arrested. Fred committed suicide while awaiting trial, but Rose was convicted and sentenced to a whole life term. Later, 25 Cromwell Street was demolished to deter inappropriate tourist attention.

I remember a beautiful sight of the comet Shoemaker-Levy, over the Welsh mountains, when Gareth and I were returning to Brecon one evening and again when we were visiting Glyn and Nicki in Pangbourne. Comets are objects in space consisting mainly of ice. They have long tails pointing directly away from the Sun, positioned by the Solar Wind. The comet was orbiting Jupiter, which it finally crashed into, ejecting debris and providing scientists with information from which they could make many calculations regarding the composition of Jupiter.

In a sense, 1994 was the year Britain ceased to be an island, with the opening of the Channel Tunnel. A tunnel under the Channel had first been proposed in 1802, but technical difficulties, financial and political issues, fears of compromising national security and difficulties in providing connections which could cope at each end had always prevented it from becoming a reality. Construction began in 1988, and it has the longest underwater section of any tunnel in the world. It provides passenger rail, road and freight rail services, and by 2017 was comparable to Dover for cross-channel transport.

We had another lovely family Christmas in Brecon before Christmas, and just after Christmas on 28th December, Nicki gave birth to Oliver Jack Jones.

I was teaching part-time at Christ College and came across an advertisement for a science competition. It involved the students doing practical and contextual research. My boys decided to investigate how surface area affected floating, so made identical shapes of various surface areas and tested how much weight each one could support before it sank. I had read of the recent discovery of a boat on the "Crannog" on Llangorse Lake, so we went to visit it and studied its design. We were selected for the County final, where the boys competed in practical tasks, a quiz and had to give an artistic presentation. I had enlisted the help of the English department, who wrote a song for the boys to perform. They were delighted to come third. The next year I entered the competition with the girls from St David's and they too reached the County final and came third.

Throughout 1995, it was obvious that St David's was struggling, and the temporary Head was due to leave at the end of the year. It was suggested that I take over. It was quite a difficult decision because I knew I could find myself out of a job in the near future. Meanwhile, Gareth had retired from teaching and offered to act as Bursar if I took the job. That was an act of love because it was a real example of a "square peg in a round hole"; however, we decided that it was worth trying to save the school, so I accepted.

Many people have heard of Fermat's Last Theorem, even if they have no idea what it is. Nowadays, it sometimes appears in quiz questions. Being called his last theorem, it has a certain air of mystery about it. He actually proposed it in 1637. It states that no three positive whole numbers a, b, c, can satisfy the equation: $a^n + b^n = c^n$ for n any greater than 2. It is easy to see that it can work for 1, since $a + b = c$, could have an infinite number of combinations, and $a^2 + b^2 = c^2$ is satisfied by some whole number combinations for a right-angled triangle, such as 3,4,5 and 5,12,13. Of course, it is more difficult to prove a negative than it is a positive, so that is perhaps why it had not been proven until Andrew Wiles came along. He first presented proof in 1993, but an error was found in it and not corrected until 1995.

From 1992 onwards, the news had frequently involved the war in Bosnia. I'm afraid I could not follow the complications of the warring factions, but it seemed that, as with so many other conflicts, it derived from a settlement after WW11 and involved territory and religious disputes, but it emerged that in 1995 at Srebrenica, Bosnian Serb forces massacred 7000 Bosnian Muslims. In the years following the war, the UN International Criminal Tribunal indicted individuals from all sides, but the most prominent was Serb President Slobodan Milosovic, accused of genocide and crimes against humanity. He died in prison before the conclusion of his trial.

Gareth and I went to the Canary Islands again between Christmas and New Year, which was a bit of a rush, since I was due to take over as Head of St David's the day after we got back, but we had booked it before I knew of the Headship. I had left all sorts of contingency plans in case we were delayed. As it happened, we were not, and I did not miss my first day. Gareth was acting as Bursar, but we were working for only one salary between us. I had no deputy head, no examinations officer, and no heads of departments. It was extremely hard work; I was not only Head of the school, but also chief executive of the business and had to be au fait with employment law, company law, charity law, health and safety legislation, safeguarding responsibilities for the boarders and much more, but at least those teachers that we had were all as dedicated as we were to try to save the school. The previous head had started a nursery school attached to the school, but it was not very well run. Gareth's middle son, Gerwyn, took over the administration and his wife Wendy, did the catering, and it became the only viable part of the school. There were only a few episodes to relieve the hard work. One was Gareth, producing a performance of "Oliver" in the Theatre in Brecon. The local theatre group provided the adults, while the school provided all the children. The school music teacher taught them the songs. Gareth directed the whole thing, and it was a tremendous success, both critically and financially. My only contribution was to do a cartwheel into the splits in the "Three Cripples" pub scene while the song "Oom-pah-pah" was being sung. Gareth's son Gethin was in Brecon at the time and was brilliant as Fagin. Mobile phones existed at this time, but they were big and bulky. We managed a night away at the caravan in

Saundersfoot, taking the school phone with us in case there was an emergency. Just after we arrived, the phone started making a beeping noise and we tried, but failed, to get in touch with the school to see if there was a problem, so we decided we must go back, it turned out that the beeping was signalling a low battery! The previous year, I had been nominated for a "Primary Science Teacher of the Year" award by the Institute of Physics, so we travelled to Liverpool for a ceremony to receive the award, which made a pleasant weekend away from work. Gethin married Sarah, and we arranged that they could have the reception in St David's with the lovely gardens.

Unfortunately, in the outside world, the news was not always so good. In Dunblane in Scotland, Thomas Hamilton opened fire at a primary school, killing sixteen pupils and one teacher and injuring fifteen other people. It was the worst mass shooting in British history and brought about two new laws outlawing handguns in private ownership, with very few exemptions.

In Afghanistan, the Taliban had emerged in 1994 and by 1996 wrested power away from the Mujahideen warlords, to rule seventy-five per cent of the country. By 2000, it was ninety per cent. The regime called itself the "Islamic Emirate of Afghanistan" but was never recognised by any country. The Taliban enforced a strict "Sharia Law" code and was widely condemned for massacring civilians, refusing to allow women to go to school or take employment and many other abuses. I was to come to know more about Afghanistan later when my son Tim, then in the HAC (Honourable Artillery Company) did two tours of Afghanistan.

To end on a more cheerful note, 1996 saw the Comprehensive Nuclear Test Ban Treaty signed by UK. USA and the Soviet Union. The first nuclear tests had been in 1945 and over the years up to 2.4 million people have died from the effects. Following years of protests from campaigns like the "Ban the bomb" with its distinctive logo, there had been a limited ban in 1963, allowing only underground tests, though not all countries signed up to it; unfortunately, the same applies to this ban – not all countries comply.

It was becoming obvious that St David's could not survive, despite our efforts. There was simply not a large enough market for it, but it was a little difficult, because as a business, bankruptcy should be declared immediately and trading ceased, but as a school, we needed to give parents a term's notice. The school finally closed at the end of the Spring term 1997. As well as coping with the legalities of closing down the school, I had obviously been looking for other jobs. There was nothing available around Brecon, so we decided to go further afield. Having done his degree in London, Gareth was delighted to have the opportunity to return to London. I would have been a little intimidated if I had not been going with Gareth. I secured a job at a prep school called Durston House for September and then a job at Kensington Prep School just for the summer term, so we moved to London.

Chapter 20
Move to London

We were lucky to secure a flat to rent in Ealing, which is where Durston House was situated, but our flat was at the top of a three-storey house, and it used to get very hot and stuffy in the evenings. The man who owned the house, converted into flats, lived downstairs. The smell of boiled cabbage pervaded the whole house. Money was tight because we still had the house in Brecon, Gareth was not earning, and we had the extra cost of the rent. We had only been moved in a couple of days when I came home to find a note from Gareth to the effect that he had had to go to Pangbourne at Glyn's urgent request to pick Oliver up from nursery because Nicki was giving birth to their daughter. Could I get the train to Pangbourne – I scarcely knew where the station was, but I made it to Pangbourne. For the summer term, I had to commute to Parson's Green, where Kensington Prep had just relocated, from central London, so they could have more space. I enjoyed teaching there, but obviously, being there for just one term, I did not get to know the girls or the staff. One morning in an assembly, I listened to the story of why the moon goes through phases – being eaten by the bad wolf and then gradually being released by the good mice. I found myself wondering what chance I stood to teach proper science when the pupils believed stories like that. In fact, when you think about it, how can you teach scientific investigation and evidence-based conclusions, when your pupils still believe the story of a man with a white beard in a red coat, flying round the world in a single night in a sledge pulled by twelve reindeer dropping presents down the chimney! I relayed all this to Gareth in the evening and reiterated the idea that we should write a series of books for four to five-year-olds, in which the science is correct. He started to say, 'That will take a lot of thinking about', but I said, 'No, I've already got it mapped out in my head.' I presented him with the main ideas the next day. He set about writing the draft of the first story. That evening, I was delighted with the draft. It was beautifully written and exactly as I had hoped. The dialogue made the characters seem real. *The Wonderful World of Suzy Squirrel* was born, followed by *Suzy Squirrel and Friends*. The books followed the topics of the Early Years curriculum and were complete with activities and teaching notes for staff. We eventually found a publisher, but it was not easy because we kept being faced with comments like; 'Oh we only publish English, not science' or, 'We publish science books not stories.'

In August, the nation and the world were shocked by the death of Princess Diana in a car crash in a French tunnel. There were numerous press reports and much speculation. The driver of the car, Henri Paul was found to be over the drink-drive limit. The other occupants of the car were Dodi Fayed and Trevor Rees-Jones, Dodi's bodyguard. None of them was wearing a seat belt. Only Trevor Rees-Jones survived. Were they speeding to avoid paparazzi? Rumours swirled for months, including conspiracy theories stoked mainly by Dodi Fayed's father, Mohamed Al-Fayed, owner of the Ritz Hotel, Paris, where they had driven from. A French investigation concluded in 1999 that the crash was caused by driving at speed and under the influence of alcohol. There was an outpouring of grief, and 2.5 billion people watched her funeral.

Chapter 21
Durston House

I started my role as Head of Science at Durston House in September 1997. Garth secured an interesting job taking tourists on very personalised tours around London. His thorough knowledge of London and English history and his "perfect English gentleman manners" impressed American visitors in particular, as did his always immaculate Jaguar. He had some very interesting characters in his car. One couple used to come over from America on the QE11 and fly back on Concorde. Unusually, Gareth did the pick-up at Heathrow and on the drive back into London, the guy said, 'I don't suppose you know a place called Stackpole; that's my name and I'm told my family came from there.' He was sitting in a car with the only man in London who would know the place – a tiny village in Wales. Although Gareth subsequently visited it and explored the church graveyard and various records, he could find no trace. They were due to get married in a castle in Scotland and then fly down to London for the evening celebration, so they had arrangements to make and would always ask for Gareth. They would fly over for her fittings at her dressmaker for her bespoke gown. On one occasion, he said, 'I need help to arrange a barge on the Thames for a medieval-themed evening, do you know where we go?' Of course, Gareth did. They went to sort it out while the fiancée was having her fitting, with Gareth sworn to secrecy. We were invited to the function. Before the event, all the guests were to go to

Burman's – the theatre costumier – and order a medieval costume. Gareth looked great in his, but I could not find anything in my size which I liked, so I adapted a green velvet gown, which I had, by adding a long train and long trailing sleeves lined with satin. We were picked up by car and taken to the wharf to join the barge, which then took a trip along the river, with Tower Bridge being opened specially and a firework display with the bridge as background. I would have loved to stay longer, but it was a weekday, and we had school the next day, so we had to be sensible and leave at a reasonable time.

At the beginning of October of that year, with the proceeds from the sale of my house in Worcester as deposit, we bought a beautiful 1-bedroom ground-floor flat in Hillcrest Road, Ealing, on top of Hanger Hill, with a swimming pool in the beautiful grounds. It was a surreal experience because when we were in the estate agent's office negotiating to buy it, he said, 'I'll see if I can contact the owner, he is often abroad.' We listened to our end of a very strange conversation, which appeared to be the owner saying, 'Not *the* Mr and Mrs Jones, from Brecon?' and then not only accepting our offer but *dropping the price by* £500. I will never forget the look on the agent's face. It turned out that the owner had four daughters at St David's. I had never really spoken to him very much, always being so busy, though I had spoken to his wife, but Gareth had chatted to him often and vaguely remembered him mentioning that he had a flat in London. While fitting out the flat, we had an instructive incident. I had bought some curtains, but later decided they were not really what I wanted. Gareth and I were sitting on the floor, looking at the curtains, still in their packet, propped up against the wall. I knew I did not like them, but thought Gareth did, so was going to go along with it. Unbeknown to me, Gareth did not like them but thought that I did, so was happy to accept them. We very nearly ended up with something neither of us liked, but just confessed in time. From that day onwards, we would always just say "Curtains" if we were about to do the same thing again.

Tobacco Companies had always played a large part in Formula 1 motorcar racing sponsorship. The success of the advertising is illustrated by the fact that in 1978, the Lotus was known not as the Lotus, but as the "JPS" (John Player Special); however, increasing knowledge of the harmful effects of smoking had caused concerns over advertising. Tony Blair's Labour Party had a ban on tobacco advertising for F1 as part of its election promises, but never followed through, perhaps after they realised how many of the F1 teams were based in the UK and the harm it would do to the economy, or perhaps it was to do with the 1-million-pound donation from Bernie Eccleston. The party was forced to hand it back in the ensuing scandal. Inevitably, over the next few years, smoking bans were gradually introduced.

Gareth and I tended to drive out of London on Sundays to find a nice spot for lunch. On one occasion, we had gone to Henley. On the way back to the car, we passed an estate agent's window. I walked past and then did a double-take and walked back. There was a beautiful villa with a pool in Spain advertised for £40,000. We began a fantasy scenario, but it was really just that – a fantasy. A few days later, back in London, we saw an advertisement for an exhibition at the local hotel about villas in Spain; it seemed an odd coincidence, so we decided to go. One company was offering a long weekend buying trip, all expenses paid for £250 each. We accepted. The only stipulation was that you had to have a two-thousand-pound bank draft to show good faith, but there was no compulsion to buy. We were shown several properties and got to the point of saying yes to one and were due to sign the contracts the next day. We were woken that night by a thunderstorm (yes, a thunderstorm in Spain). It was "Curtains" again; we each confessed to feelings of apprehension, rather than elation at the prospect of our villa in Spain. We each had a feeling that, though we had liked a lot of what we had seen, we were only shown what they wanted us to see, and there might be better choices, so we did not go through with the purchase. When we got back to London, we decided we had been rather silly; that, in fact, we did want to buy a villa in Spain; all we had done was to make it more expensive next time since it was a period in which prices were rising.

That year was my 50th birthday, so Gareth arranged a party back in Brecon. It was actually Nicki who did all the cooking, because Gareth couldn't cook, but it was a lovely celebration.

1998 began with the Clinton–Lewinsky scandal when, if like me, you had never heard of the idea before, you were introduced to "telephone sex". Bill Clinton US President denied having relations with Monica Lewinsky, a White House intern, with the statement in a TV interview, 'I did not have sexual relations with that woman, Ms Lewinsky.' Throughout the year, further revelations resulted in charges of perjury and finally to impeachment. A little later, we were interested to discover that one of the clients in Gareth's car for a London tour was Keneth Starr, who had been a prosecutor in the case against Clinton.

Gareth and I went back to Spain. Glyn had a contact who worked in Spain, so we got in touch with an estate agent through him. This time, we did not feel we were being shown only what they wanted us to see. The villa we agreed to buy was unfinished, but since we were getting to know Spanish ways, we decided that even though completion would be during the Easter holidays, we would not go to take possession until the summer holidays, so as to be sure that delays would not cause us a wasted journey. The purchase price was in pesetas, so it seemed to be an awful lot of them.

On 24 February, Sarah gave birth to her and Gethin's daughter, Agnelle.

I remember seeing reports of the War in Kosovo, but found it very confusing as to who was fighting whom and why. I eventually understood that the KLA (Kosovo Liberation Army) was fighting a Yugoslavian (Serbia and Montenegro) attempt to expel ethnic Albanians by abuse and repression. The fighting ended the next year after NATO (North Atlantic Treaty Organisation) intervened with a controversial bombing campaign, and the Yugoslav and Serbian forces withdrew from Kosovo.

We flew to Spain immediately after we finished school, and sure enough, the villa was not quite finished, but it was enough to enable us to move in, so we were happy. We overlapped for a few days with Glyn and Nicki, then returned to UK.

One news story I was particularly appalled by was the saga of Andrew Wakefield, a doctor who claimed his research showed a link between the MMR (measles, mumps and rubella.) vaccine and autism. It was later shown that the work was not just flawed but actually fraudulent. He was later struck off the medical register in the UK. He resigned from his post at the Royal Free Hospital in 2001 and moved to the USA but continued to be an anti-vaccine activist and earned a living giving talks and seminars. The result was a lowering of the uptake of the vaccine and an increase in deaths from measles, all due to his fraudulent research results.

The "Good Friday Agreement" finally brought an end to the

unrest and violence known as "The Troubles" due to ethnic, religious and political differences in Northern Ireland, which had been going on since the 1960s. It was enacted between most of the Northern Irish political parties and the British and Irish governments and is the basis of the Northern Ireland devolved system of government today.

India caused global uproar by undertaking nuclear tests, negating the optimism of the 1996 Comprehensive Treaty, to which India was not a signatory. Not surprisingly, Pakistan also carried out tests, because the antipathy between India and Pakistan had not abated. There was a great state of unease at the thought that two warring neighbours could both have nuclear capability.

Relations between Pakistan and the USA were further strained due to their apparent support for al-Qaeda. In August, simultaneous bomb attacks occurred at US Embassies in Nairobi, Kenya and Dar-es-Salaam, Tanzania. 224 people were killed and 4,500 injured. I took particular interest in the news since I had been to both cities to visit my then finance in 1970. The USA was determined to trace the perpetrators, and 900 FBI agents travelled widely to gather information. Al-Qaeda was quickly identified, with Osama Bin Laden being the main culprit. Altogether, twenty people have been indicted, and seven are serving life sentences in the USA.

I have just read that two American astronauts may have to stay on the International Space Station until next year, following a fault in the Boeing Starliner. The prolonged stay could have life-changing effects on their bodies, such as loss of bone density and muscle atrophy. The first parts for the ISS were taken up in 1998. 5 international space agencies USA, Russia, Europe, Japan and Canada are involved in the project, which sees the station orbiting the Earth sixteen times a day. It is quite an unusual example of international cooperation. The aim is to carry out research, much of which cannot be performed on Earth. 270 astronauts from twenty countries have visited the station.

Despite the fact that homosexuality was no longer illegal, an incident occurred which showed there was still a lot of suspicion and prejudice surrounding the subject. Ron Davies defeated Rhodri Morgan to become Labour's candidate for First Secretary of the Welsh assembly, but a month later, it was reported that he had been mugged on Clapham Common. At first, he was seen as the victim, but Clapham Common is a known meeting place for gays. It emerged that he had agreed "to go for a meal" with a man he had met. Full details have never emerged, but amid much speculation, he resigned, citing "A moment of madness". He later admitted to being bisexual.

On January 1st 1999, the euro was introduced to the financial markets as an accounting currency, though physical coins and banknotes were not in use until 2002. Even though the UK was in the EU, the euro was not adopted as UK currency. At that time, we were exchanging money to go to Spain at the rate of 1.50€ to £1. It is now about 1.15.

I have always admired Leonardo da Vinci, so was delighted to hear that after years of deterioration and damage, the twenty-year restoration of the "The Last Supper" had been completed, though of course, it was controversial – some critics complaining that so much had been removed, that it was scarcely the work of Da Vinci anymore.

In March, a truck, carrying flour and margarine, caught fire half-way through the Mont Blanc Tunnel between France and Italy. Other vehicles also caught fire and emergency vehicles had difficulty getting to the scene. 39 people died and the incident caused major changes to be made to the tunnel. Safety procedures were also reviewed for the Channel Tunnel.

Gerwyn and Wendy welcomed their son Gwyn.

The whole nation was shocked by the death of Jill Dando, a very popular TV presenter for the BBC. Presenting programmes such as: "Breakfast-time", "The six O'clock News" and "Crimewatch". She was shot dead by a single bullet to the head on her own front doorstep in broad daylight. A neighbour found her about fifteen minutes after the shooting. Barry George, a known sex offender, was charged with murder, convicted and spent eight years in prison, but was then exonerated. This is Britain's highest-profile unsolved murder. There have been many theories ranging from someone from her "Crimewatch" programme wanting revenge to a random act of violence; some of which were explored in a BBC programme on the 20th anniversary of the crime, and a three-part Netflix series. One of the longest-lasting theories is of a Serbian hitman. Jill had been prominent in reporting on the Kosovo War. The circumstances of the shooting: by a single shot to the head; on her doorstep; in broad daylight; with the perpetrator escaping almost unseen, seemed to have the hallmarks of a professional, but the police's chief suspect was able to prove he was not in the country at the time of the shooting. Twenty-five years on the case is still unsolved.

Chapter 22
A New Millennium

December 31st. 1999 was popularly called Millennium eve and 2000 was the start of the 21st century, though technically it could be argued that 2000 is the last year of the 20th century.

There had been dire predictions as to what would happen at midnight on Millennium Eve; that the whole computer network would collapse, because the systems had been set up to deal with 2-digit dates e.g. 00 for 1900 and so could not cope with 2000, or that terrorists would take the opportunity to spread a fatal computer virus. Many of our family were gathered at the house of Nicki's sister in Cornwall. She and her husband were artists and had a large "old schoolhouse", perfect for partying. At midnight, we went outside to launch fireworks, but we were concerned when the rockets failed to rise and landed on the roof of a house further down the hill; fortunately, no harm came of it.

Although he was seen as holding mainly traditional views of the doctrine of the Catholic Church, and could be expected to defend the Church at all costs, Pope John Paul II apologised to individuals and organisations, including for sexual abuse by Catholic priests. In the "Great Jubilee" year of 2000, in a prayer for forgiveness of the sins of the Catholic Church, he apologised for transgressions as far-reaching as to Galileo Galilei for his house arrest for his views on the Sun-centric Universe; for the Atlantic Slave trade and failure of the Church to take any action during the holocaust.

I often visited the Science Museum, and I remember there being a Leonardo de Vinci exhibition, including the design of a parachute because Adrian Nicholas had built a parachute from the design and showed that it worked. Leonardo designed many items way ahead of his time, including a crossbow.

At Durston, I became aware that when the boys left at twelve years old to go to their next school, they had to make choices as to subjects to take. One such choice was whether or not to take CDT (Craft, Design and Technology), but they had never done any CDT, so how could they make such a choice? I suggested to the Head that we should introduce the subject, but he said there was no time on the timetable, so I said, 'We can take two lessons from Science.' He was horrified until I assured him that I could do that and still maintain results, which I did. One of my proudest moments was when two of my boys were awarded A* in the entrance exams for St Paul's – two of only four awarded amongst all the candidates.

I was devasted to hear of the crash of Concorde shortly after take-off from Paris on a flight to New York, killing all 109 on board and four on the ground. It was caused by a piece of debris on the runway blowing a tyre, which then flew up and ruptured a fuel tank. I felt a particular affinity with Concorde because my father had panelled the cowling adaptation to the Vulcan, for the testing of the Rolls Royce engine for Concorde, and Gareth's middle son, Gerwyn, was working at Heath Row and saw the plane every day, as did we, since our flat in Ealing was almost under the flight path. I loved watching the majestic silhouette. This was the only fatal crash in the plane's twenty-seven-year operational history and the plane's safety record was better than any other plane, but the whole fleet was grounded and after a brief reintroduction was retired.

News programmes were full of the news of the explosion aboard the Russian Kursk submarine and its subsequent sinking to the seabed 108m below, during a naval exercise in the Barents Sea. The submarine had an almost mythical reputation as being unsinkable and being able to withstand a direct hit from a torpedo. As usual, the Russians misled the World with misinformation and understatement and although the response was criticised as slow and inept, and they refused help from other countries' ships. It is unlikely that the British and Norwegian divers who were eventually allowed access would have found anyone alive, as subsequent investigation showed that the submariners would have been dead after about six hours.

Al-Qaeda claimed responsibility for the suicide bomb attack on the USS Cole while it was being refuelled in Yemen. Seventeen US Navy sailors were killed and thirty-seven were injured. It was claimed that al-Qaeda could not have carried out the attacks without the collusion of the Sudanese government, but it was many years before frozen Sudanese assets were paid to the relatives of those killed.

The country was shocked by the conviction of GP Dr Harold Shipman on murder charges – the only doctor ever to have been convicted of murder in the UK. Some estimates put the number of people he killed between 1975 and 1998 as high as 250. In 1998, concerns had been raised about the abnormally high death rate among his elderly patients, but it was 2000 before enough evidence had been collected. His motives have never really been explained, but there is a suggestion that he was influenced by the death of his mother when he was seventeen, when a doctor prescribed morphine for pain relief from her cancer. Another theory is that it was purely for profit since some of the patients changed their wills. When police found £10,000 worth of jewellery in his garage in 2005, it provided another possible motive. He hanged himself in his cell in 2004. There are two legacies of the case: numerous changes to procedures by the BMA (British Medical Association), such as procedures for certifying a death and authorising a cremation, and a memorial to the victims in Hyde Park, called "the Garden of Tranquillity".

With the arrival of the grandchildren, we had decided that nobody's house was big enough for family celebrations, so we had taken to booking a hotel for the weekend. In 2001, we celebrated our 10th wedding anniversary with a party in Bristol, and not too long afterwards, Gerwyn and Wendy had their daughter Megan.

Of course, the whole year's news was dominated by the 11th September attack on the Twin Towers. I remember walking into the staff room at Durston to find all the staff arranged round the TV, horrified at the unfolding disaster. Nineteen terrorists hijacked four commercial airliners. The first two were crashed into the Twin Towers at the World Trade Centre in New York; the third crashed into the Pentagon, but the fourth crashed into a field in Pennsylvania, following a revolt by brave passengers. 2,977 people were killed. The hijackings changed our experience of air travel, as countries around the world introduced measures such as the limits on quantities of liquids in cabin baggage and scanners. The USA responded by declaring a global war on terror and countries which harboured terrorists, including Afghanistan, Iraq and Syria. The US led a multinational invasion of Afghanistan, but Osama bin Laden escaped into the White Mountains. He denied any involvement until 2004, but then accepted responsibility for the attacks and attempted to justify them. He was eventually killed in 2011 in his compound in Abbottabad, Pakistan. The war in Afghanistan went on for another eight years.

I had applied for a post at Godolphin and Latymer school for September and was accepted, but the Head of Durston said he would have difficulty in replacing me and so would not release me until the end of the Autumn term; fortunately, Godolphin and Latymer were prepared to wait until then.

Chapter 23
Godolphin and Latymer

As I started at Godolphin, they were making preparations to perform "Vackees" in the theatre in Hammersmith. I got involved in making some of the costumes. I had come across the play when I was at Kensington Prep School, but until then, I had no idea that children had been evacuated from London during WW II, separated from their parents for several years. I suppose that was a consequence of living in the Midlands and not having TV. The play is funny, but also moving. Sometime later, my grandson Oliver had a history project to do over the summer holiday. He interviewed his other grandfather and videoed it. It transpired that Phil had been one of the children evacuated from London, so it was a very poignant and instructive story. It was a shame that Ollie's history teacher did not find time to show the video.

Tim, who had always been very adventurous, had set off on a yacht across the Atlantic, and we had heard little of him for quite a while. When he resurfaced, it was as a firefighter in Greenwich. A colleague at Godolphin said, 'Oh, that must be every mother's nightmare,' to which I replied, 'Oh no, it's one of the least dangerous things he has done.'

Perhaps because we spent so much time in Spain and were used to high summer temperatures, it largely passed us by that 2002 was the hottest year since 1998. In fact, the next year turned out to be its equal.

Following the 9/11 attacks of the year before, international relations were dominated by the universal need to combat terrorism. Several agreements and treaties were signed, but there were still thirty-one recognised armed conflicts, notably India and Pakistan over the disputed region of Kashmir. The world was apprehensive, once again, at the prospect of warring neighbours with nuclear capability.

In Iraq, Saddam Hussein continued to fail to cooperate with weapons inspectors and the term "Weapons of mass destruction" (WMD) was heard more and more frequently on the news. The then Prime Minister, Tony Blair, was convinced that Saddam Hussein DID have WMD and used his certainty to justify sending British troops into Iraq. A few years later, the Chilcot report would stop short of accusing Blair of lying to Parliament but did assert that intelligence was misinterpreted and that too little thought had been given to what would be the aftermath if Saddam Hussein were toppled.

A US-led coalition, including UK, Austria and Poland invaded Iraq, with the stated aims of destroying WMD, which it claimed were an immediate threat to world peace, ending Iraq's support for terrorism and freeing the Iraqi people. The war was always controversial, both in the UK and the US, with some argument that invasion would increase, not decrease, global instability. No WMDs were found. Hussein went into hiding but was captured in December of that year.

Although we were living in London, Gareth was still in touch with the Talgarth Male Voice Choir. That year their chosen "tour" venue was Torrevieja, Spain, which is very close to our village of San Miguel. I persuaded Gareth that he should go, even though I couldn't because I was working. He did not sing, since he had not been rehearsing with them, but he went to the concerts and visited their hotel. He invited some of his friends to the villa for a swim and to laze by the pool one afternoon. On the last evening, they were all due to meet up for dinner at an outdoor restaurant on the seafront. Gareth arrived, but for quite a while no one turned up. He was just getting anxious when they finally arrived, with a story to tell. Apparently, there had been a spate of robberies from hotel rooms in the area for quite some time. As the singers were exiting their rooms, they came face-to-face with a robber brandishing a knife. One of the choir members, an ex-rugby player, tackled him and brought him down. The local police were very pleased as they finally arrested the whole gang, and there was an article in the local paper. With typical modesty, Di said to Gareth, 'Mind you, Gary, nobody ever got past me on the blindside!' It couldn't be more of a clique of Welshness – singing and rugby!

We held Gareth's 65th birthday party in "La Tasca", a Spanish restaurant in Ealing, with all five grandchildren there.

In 2004, a year after the invasion of Iraq, Kofi Annan, the UN secretary general declared the war illegal and a breach of the UN charter. Al-Qaeda continued to be a problem, with an attack on Cercanias trains in Madrid, which killed 192 people. The US-led coalition in Iraq handed over to the Iraqi interim government, and preliminary investigations began in preparation for the trial of Saddam Hussein for war crimes and crimes against humanity. The trial would begin in the next year.

Most people were shocked by the news of the Beslan School siege. Chechen rebels took 1,128 people, mostly children, hostage in a school at Beslan in Russia. They were demanding that Russia withdraw from and recognise the independence of Chechnya. I remember thinking, *No matter what their cause, what sort of people use children as pawns?* The siege ended when Russian security forces stormed the building. Around 330 people were killed. The contrast with the storming of the Iranian Embassy, where only one hostage was killed, struck me forcibly.

I think 2004 was the first time I had heard the word "Tsunami" used, though it had been current for quite some time. Broadcasters often refer to tsunamis as tidal waves, though, in fact, they are not related to tides at all. They have their origin in large bodies of water being displaced, such as following an earthquake or volcanic eruption. Although Japan has the longest recorded history of tsunamis, this one, originating in the Indian Ocean, was one of the most devastating. Around 230,000 people died.

In Britain, the Civil Partnership Act gave equal rights to same-sex couples as to married couples. Initially, it was defined only in terms of same-sex couples but later was extended to opposite-sex couples.

The UK (and the rest of the world) became aware of the relationship between Prince William, heir to the throne, and Katherine Middleton, when they were photographed on a ski-trip. They had met and become friends while at university in St Andrew's and then became housemates.

Tim was by now racing a motorcycle and sidecar combination, and we went to see him at Brand's Hatch; unfortunately, he had a high-speed accident; fortunately, he was not too badly hurt. The other driver in the collision had his license revoked because the accident was his fault. A few years later, Tim was driving sports cars at events and open days. At one such at Cheltenham racecourse, he met Suzie, the marketing manager.

Over the years, as the family grew, hotels had been getting more and more expensive, and more and more restrictive of what they would allow, e.g. children in the dining room, so I explored the possibilities of renting a large house. I would have loved a castle, with a hallway, grand staircase and a huge log fire, but they were all situated in Scotland, so I found more central venues since Ger and Wendy were based in Carmarthenshire, Gethin and Sarah in central Wales, Glyn and Nicki in Berkshire, Tim, Steve and Gareth and I in London.

It does not often snow in London, but one day I was teaching a group of 6th form girls when they became increasingly aware of snowflakes falling past the window. They became more and more distracted until I said, 'Oh, for goodness' sake, go and open the window, stick your heads out, put your tongues out to taste it if you want to, then we can get on with the lesson.' As she went across to the window, one of them said, 'I know, Mrs Jones, seventeen going on five, but I was six the last time it snowed.' She was quite right – it had not snowed in London for eleven years.

One of the benefits of living in a place like London is the opportunity to see ceremonials such as the trooping of the colour, but equally striking, though less grand, are the Fiestas for which Spain is famous. Even a little village like San Miguel has its event, with processions publicised in posters, translated, to our amusement, as containing "long-shanked fire-eaters". They turned out to be stilt walkers juggling with firebrands. We took the opportunity to visit some of Spain's famous cities, such as Seville, Cordoba and Granada, though we encountered a cyclone in Seville and had to shelter as the gargoyles were crashing onto the pavement from the Cathedral.

Perhaps if a modern youngster were asked when YouTube was launched, they would say in the "olden days", but, in fact, it was 2005. Apparently, the first video was "Me at the Zoo"!

I remember Gareth and I were travelling back through Spain when Prince Charles married Camilla Parker-Bowles and we saw it broadcast on Spanish TV. There had been controversy about his relationship with Camilla throughout his marriage to Diana and many people found it hard to accept her. There was much debate about whether she should be allowed to be queen when Charles acceded to the throne, but I think she has shown herself to be a hardworking Royal and a great support to the now King Charles.

There was still trouble in the middle East. One of the holiest sites in Shia Islam, the al-Askari Shrine, was attacked, resulting in full-scale war in Iraq, which lasted until 2008. Hamas fired rockets into Israel, to which Israel responded with an offensive in Gaza, from which they had withdrawn the year before.

There were several interesting scientific developments, which I remember hearing about. The human genome project was fulfilled by the final sequencing. Pluto was downgraded to a dwarf planet. I remember there was a time when I was teaching my pupils there were ten planets, not nine (though I had to warn them that for exam purposes they must quote nine) because I had read about the recent discovery of a planet beyond Pluto. Now, apparently, new definitions of what constituted a planet had been agreed by the scientific community, and Pluto was deemed too small to be called a planet, so we are back to eight planets orbiting our Sun. The Cassini-Huygens spacecraft reported evidence that suggested there might be water on one of Saturn's moons. My pupils would often ask me if I believed there was life on other planets (usually when they wanted a distraction from what we were supposed to be studying.), and I think they were surprised when I said, 'Yes, of course there is, but not in our Solar System. No other planet in our system has the right conditions for life, but there are billions of stars in our Galaxy, just like our Sun and billions of Galaxies. It is statistically almost certain that some of them have systems with a planet with the right conditions. Nowadays, we have evidence of planets around other stars beyond our galaxy and increasing evidence that there might once have been water on various moons of planets in our system.'

There has always been news of hurricanes, particularly in certain regions at certain times of the year, but in some years, if they make landfall in highly populated or vulnerable areas, they are more significant than at other times. This was one such when Hurricane Katrina hit the Gulf Coast. A thousand people lost their lives.

There was a UN Climate Change Conference in Montreal. Climate change had been on the syllabus for teaching in schools for a few years, but there was nothing like as much information as there is now. In fact, it was still really only a theory, and there was a great deal of rhetoric and speculation. I went to an excellent exhibition in the Science Museum, which laid out the evidence in a very clear way. After all, temperature records only began in about 1850 and the Earth has been here for 4.5 billion years, so the significance of changes was not obvious. The Earth has gone through several periods of cooling and warming, nothing to do with human activity. There are many factors involved, and unfortunately, the media are often guilty of oversimplifying to the point of inaccuracy, but it is now largely agreed that in the post-industrial era, human activity is significantly affecting average global temperatures. One factor is the so-called "greenhouse effect", which shows a mechanism by which gases in the atmosphere might contribute to warming. Burning fossil fuels emits these gases into the atmosphere, which is why I am more convinced than ever that while alternative sources of energy such as wind, wave and biomass are important, their main contribution will be to buy time for mankind to master nuclear fusion.

Chapter 24
Retirement

I retired from Godolphin in July, and we went to Spain until November. Being there for a longer period meant that I could get more involved in activities, so I joined a tap dance group. Ella had shown an interest in performing, so when we were back in the UK, I asked her if she would like to learn to tap dance. She and I performed a routine to "American Patrol" at the family Christmas. I saw an advertisement for a teacher needed just for the Spring term at Camden School for Girls, so I went back just for the one term, four days a week.

Almost everyone was touched by the global financial crisis in 2007. A friend of mine had started his own business, which had been successful until the onset of the crisis, but then the increasing closures of his customers gave him problems. His business survived, just – but was not the income stream it should have been. The crisis was largely caused by the "Subprime Mortgage" crisis in the US. Subprime means less than ideal and ill-advised lending led to the collapse of the housing market and, as a knock-on effect, a global financial crisis, which went on into 2008 and the bankruptcy of Lehman Brothers, a major mortgage lender. Another knock-on effect was the decline in pension investment funds, which ultimately led to the raising of the state pension age in the UK.

While Tim had been in the Army Air Corps, he had learned to fly a helicopter, so he took it up again and took his pilot's licence. Gwyn and Megan were delighted when we arranged for Tim to take them up for a surprise helicopter flight. At one point after being told what was going to happen, Gwyn was rather quiet, so we asked him if there was anything wrong. He said, 'Oh no, I'm just trying not to be annoying. Actually, I want to jump up and down and shout.'

Now that Gareth and I were both retired, we were able to be more adventurous. I had always wanted to go to the Galapagos Islands, where Darwin formulated his ideas on evolution, so in 2007, we decided that this was the best time to go. The ten-hour flight from Heathrow was a bit of a trial for Gareth, as a smoker, and changing planes in Miami was not pleasant. Ever since 9/11, the Americans had had heightened levels of security, and the guards at Miami were very intimidating, even though we were not even leaving the airport, just changing planes. We flew to Quito in Ecuador, the second-highest capital in the world and stayed two nights. It was a lovely experience, though we were fascinated by the ceiling of the restaurant where we went to eat the first night, which consisted of doors – all different designs and types. The views around Quito were amazing, but we had been warned to take care because the sun was stronger and the oxygen level lower because of the altitude. From there, we flew to Guayaquil and changed planes again to arrive at Santa Cruz to join our ship for the cruise around the islands.

The Galapagos are a group of islands sitting on the equator. The geology of the islands is remarkable. They are on the Galapagos Triple Junction; on the Nazca plate, which is moving East/Southeast and sinking under the South American plate and atop a mantle plume creating volcanoes; thus, the islands are spreading away from the centre. The older islands have completely different conditions from the younger central islands, which is what fascinated Darwin when he visited the islands. He noticed that there are differences between species on different islands, particularly the finches, whose beaks varied depending on the terrain and vegetation on each island. His observations and notes formed the basis for his *On the Origin of Species*.

Breakfast was at six thirty am. each day, after which we left the ship on rubber boats called "zodiacs" to visit that day's island. We visited Santa Cruz, Bartolome, Isabela, Fernandina, Española, Rabida and North Seymour before returning to Santa Cruz to fly home. I loved seeing all the exotic creatures including iguanas, frigate birds, blue-footed boobies, and flightless cormorants. We were surprised that the islands are home to the only penguins not in Antarctica – the cool waters of the Humboldt current allow them to thrive. Of course, we were introduced to the Galapagos tortoises, and to the breeding programme, made famous by "Lonesome George" – the last remaining Pinta Island tortoise. He was in fact, not all that lonely, since he did have other tortoises with him, but they were not the same species. He died in 2012. The second half of the cruise was marred slightly for us, by the arrival of President Bush's daughter and a large entourage, which meant heavy security by self-important bodyguards, part of the ship closed to other passengers, and the commandeering of many of the zodiacs. We also detected that cabins had been searched. On our flight home, we were held for about four hours in security in Miami with no access to water or facilities and when we were finally allowed to leave, we were given no explanation. I am not keen to visit Miami again.

William and Kate separated that year, for the second time, having broken up briefly in 2003. They were reconciled, but it would be another three years before William proposed to Kate and the press unkindly christened her "Waity Katie".

We had our own marriage saga as Tim married Suzie at Eastnor Castle – a flying arrival in a helicopter – spectacular, but difficult for the bridal dress. It took all of best man Steve's skill to help her out onto the lawn.

Since it was my 60th birthday, I imitated the queen; in having an official birthday as well as an actual one. We held a celebration for friends in Spain in the summer, then another celebration when we were back in UK in December.

At the L.H.C (Large Hadron Collider) at CERN, the European Organisation for Nuclear Research on the Franco-Swiss border, the proton beam was being used for the first time. I was particularly interested because I knew that some physicists from the Oxford physics department were involved.

There were two major natural disasters that year: Cyclone Nargis in Myanmar killing 138, 000 people and an earthquake in Sichan Province in China, which killed 87,000.

2008 was a busy year for me and Gareth, and our family. Gareth had told me about his father, who had volunteered for the RAF when WWII broke out. He was finally accepted, even though he had a wife and young child. Gareth knew that he had been stationed at Lossiemouth, but that was all he knew. Following a late-night conversation, I determined to find out more. It was a struggle at first, but finally, stretching my internet skills to the limit, I found out some information and arranged a visit to RAF Lossiemouth. We were introduced to a wonderful sergeant, who was curating a museum chronicling the war from the stories of ordinary people, not the big well-known stories. Gareth learned that his father had been killed coming back to the airfield over the golf course at the end of a training flight, when the Lancaster crashed, not far short of the runway. We were able to see the spot where it happened and view a memorial from the people of Lossiemouth to all who had lost their lives. Gareth got to sit in the cockpit of a Tornedo and talk to a pilot about to fly out to the Gulf. Gareth's life would have been very different if his father had not been killed. His father could well have been a concert singer, with all the fame and fortune that would have brought, instead of the struggle which his mother had.

We finally managed to go to Egypt and had a wonderful cruise down the Nile, flying to Abu Simbel to see the sun rise and visit the Temples of Rameses II and Nefertari. Remarkably, the temples had been moved block by block in 1968 to avoid the rising waters when the Aswan dam was built. We visited the Valley of the Kings and Karnak, among other things, but were not able to include the Pyramids and the Sphinx.

We were invited back as guests of honour to the 40th Anniversary Ball of the Oxford University Dancesport Club, which I had started while at Oxford – only then it was called the Oxford University Ballroom Dance Club. I was delighted to see how the Club was prospering.

We held an Os party to celebrate the fact that several members of the family had big birthdays: Gareth 70; Me 60 the previous December; Sarah 40; Steve 30; Agnelle 10.

I had been dancing Flamenco with a group in Torrevieja, and the family decided they would like to learn, so, at the Family Christmas celebration, we had not only all the girls, but Gareth, Steve, Ollie and Gwyn as well. I made costumes for the girls and red cummerbunds for the boys for us to dance "Sevillana". The dance consists of four "Coplas" – sections of dance getting progressively more complicated. The boys and Megan just danced the first one, Ella, Angelle and I did one and two, Ella and I did three, and I finished with four. Another performance at the celebration was *The Simpsons* written by Gareth and practised and performed by the grandchildren. Megan was only 7, so at one point Ella was to prompt her with her line "$E = mc^2$". Ella forgot to remind her, so Megan turned to Ella and said, 'You're supposed to remind me to say "$E = mc^2$".'

For Gareth's 70th birthday, his sons Gerwyn and Glyn had given him a voucher for a flight in a Tiger Moth, but it was not until 2009 that the weather forecasts made it sensible to drive from London to Gloucester to take the flight. Gareth loved it and even took the controls for the latter part of the trip. It is a pity that he never had the time or situation to pursue flying as a hobby.

By now we had been spending a lot of time in Spain each year, leaving the London flat unoccupied, so we discussed the idea of renting it out for the Summer. We managed to coordinate it just right and signed a rental agreement two days before we flew to Spain. The idea was to retrieve the flat at the end of the 6 months. In fact, the tenant wanted to stay after the six months, so we decided it made sense to let him stay on, while we rented a flat for the next six months, to avoid the hassle of having to find another tenant next spring. We rented in Cheltenham, because by now both Tim and Steve were there, which was convenient and also cost less than the rental income we were getting for the London flat.

For the family Christmas, Megan, Agnelle, Ella and I performed a tap routine to "Cabaret". Ella and I had first performed a tap routine in 2006, but this was Megan and Agnelle's first time. For Christmas Day itself, Gareth, I, Tim and Susie went out for a very nice lunch because Tim was likely to be deployed to Afghanistan shortly afterwards, so he wanted us all to have a hassle-free Christmas day.

In the USA, Eric Garner, an unarmed black man, was killed by an NYPD officer using a prohibited chokehold. He and other officers had accused Garner of selling single cigarettes from packs without tax stamps and tried to arrest him. The whole scene was captured on video and gained worldwide attention. Despite a medical examiner's verdict of homicide, the decision was taken not to indict the officer. This caused widespread unrest and protests against police brutality. The incident is often cited as a factor in the creation of the BLM, "Black Lives Matter" movement.

Like many people, I enjoyed the film *Sully*, based on the crash of Flight 1549, which occurred in 2009. The Airbus A320 had suffered a bird strike shortly after take-off and lost all power. The pilot, Chesley "Sully" Sullenberger, glided the plane to a landing on the Hudson River in downtown Manhattan, and everyone on board survived. The film portrays how he was first hailed as a hero, but then vilified when a simulator investigation showed that he could have turned back to La Guardia had he done so immediately after the strike. He was later exonerated when it was proved that the simulation did not take all real-life facts into consideration.

Chapter 25
Life in Spain

During our time in Cheltenham, we considered the option of moving to Spain permanently. We had been spending 6 months in UK and six months in Spain, hoping for the best of both worlds, but we decided that it was not really working and that we should either live in UK and holiday in Spain or live in Spain and holiday in UK – we opted for the latter. Once again, we managed to get the timings right and completed the sale of the London flat just before we were due to make the final move to Spain, in May 2010. The London flat sold for a very good price, and we were able to buy a house in Cheltenham, which we rented out to Steve, and have money to give a gift to each of the boys. We obtained residency in Spain. The tax position was a little complex, since, despite the general principle of taxation in the country of residence, our teachers' pensions were classed as government pensions and taxed at source in the UK., whereas our state pensions, investments and any other income were to be taxed in Spain. There is a "dual taxation agreement" which means you do not have to pay tax twice, but it is not simple. You have to declare all income to the Spanish authorities; they then work out what Spanish tax would be due on all of it and deduct anything you have paid in the UK. I was still writing and editing for "Curriculum Press" doing A-level Physics Factsheets – a series of revision materials for students. Of course, the position was further complicated by the fact that the Spanish tax year is

January to January, whereas UK is April to April.

We were lucky that our flights were not affected by the Icelandic ash cloud, but most travellers in Western Europe that year will remember the disruption. A series of eruptions from a volcano I can neither pronounce nor spell began in April and continued through May and June, creating the ash cloud. It was not declared as over until October, after 3 months of inactivity.

The iPad was released by Apple, though it was to be replaced by iPad2 as early as 2011. Instagram was launched for ios and rapidly gained popularity with one million registered users in two months. Although often admired for its success, it has been criticised for adversely affecting teens' mental health and not doing enough to prevent illegal and inappropriate content.

Many people were already aware of "WikiLeaks", a publisher of leaked documents, founded by Julian Assange in 2006. Julian Assange was a controversial Australian editor, publisher and activist. WikiLeaks was relaunched in 2010. Footage was leaked of the 2007 US airstrikes in Iraq, which Assange labelled "Collateral Murder". Although Assange and WikiLeaks have been commended for exposing corruption in many parts of the World, it has also been criticised for violating personal privacy, publishing e.g., medical records, social security numbers and credit card numbers. It has also been accused of bias and of nurturing conspiracy theories, and it has been claimed that some leaks have endangered the lives of serving military personnel. During 2010, there was much internal dissent and concerns about security at WikiLeaks. In November, Sweden issued a European arrest warrant for Assange over allegations of sexual assault. After a failed appeal, he sought asylum in the embassy of Ecuador in London, where he remained until 2019. After disputes with the Ecuadorian government, his asylum was rescinded, and UK police arrested him. He was sentenced to fifty weeks for bail offences and remained in Belmarsh prison until 2024, when he finally made a plea bargain with the US and was allowed to return to Australia.

The so-called "Arab Spring" began in Tunisia. A series of anti-government protests and rebellions spread across Arab countries, Libya, Egypt, Yemen and Syria; initially inspired as a demonstration against corruption and economic stagnation. Despite the hope that the protests would end corruption and increase political participation, they were largely met with violent responses by the authorities and full-scale conflict and, in some cases, regime change followed. Although the initial rebellions faded by 2012, there are conflicts all over the Arab world today, which could be said to have their roots in the Arab spring.

After her "Annus horribilis" of 1992, the queen must have been delighted when Prince William finally proposed to Kate and they announced their engagement.

During the Summer, Gareth and I visited Aitano animal park, a little to the north of us in San Miguel. It involved a coach ride around the park, stopping at various points to see the animals, wandering around (except for the lions, of course, they were in an enclosure). We were amused by the sight of a hippo being fed – the keeper lobbed a whole watermelon towards the hippo, and it opened its mouth wide and caught the melon. Chomp! The melon disappeared, to be replaced by red liquid dribbling down either side of its mouth. It looked for all the world as if the hippo was eating some poor creature alive. I took a picture of it, which we put to good use at the family Christmas as a "Caption" competition. I think the winning caption was "Hippos have no table manners". The entertainment that year consisted of me doing a Charleston, Gareth and I doing an Argentine tango, and Gwyn doing a Louis Armstrong rendition of "Hello Dolly" accompanied by all the grandchildren dancing. Meg performed some "magic" – simple, but impressive, chemical reactions.

By 2011, there was still strife in parts of the world, with the Arab spring still affecting the Middle East, but India and Bangladesh were finally able to end their demarcation dispute after forty years.

The word "tsunami" hit the news again, with an event originating from an earthquake of 9.1 in Japan. 20,000 died and 2500 were missing. Four nuclear power stations declared emergencies, and, the Fukushima station released contaminants into the air.

On 29th April, William and Kate were married at Westminster Abbey. Everything about the day was stunning, and about two billion people worldwide watched the proceedings.

We had our cause to celebrate as Gethin and Sarah renewed their wedding vows for their 15th Wedding anniversary at a tiny chapel on Rhodes, but the journey to get there was a nightmare. Gareth and I were delayed in Birmingham overnight, and when we finally took off, the pilot welcomed us to the flight to Thessaloniki! I don't think many people on the plane realised that Thessaloniki is in northern Greece, over a thousand km from our destination of Rhodes. The pilot came back on and apologised that we appeared not to have been informed of the diversion. We should have been there the day before and had time to settle in, but we only just made it to the restaurant where we were due to have dinner with Gethin, Sarah and Agnelle before it closed at eleven p.m. Gareth and I, too, celebrated an anniversary, our 20th, but not in quite such a grand way as Gethin and Sarah; we just had a party at the Castillo de Conesa just outside San Miguel.

The family Christmas saw me performing a Sevillana to "La Bahia" and Gwyn doing a hilarious karaoke with his back to the audience and a facemask on the back of his head. We spent Christmas with Steve at 229, Swindon Rd. Cheltenham and New Year's Eve with Gethin and Sarah in Nelson in Wales.

At the beginning of 2012, since we liked to holiday on cruise ships, we took particular interest in the saga of the Costa Concordia, a cruise liner, which struck a rock off the coast of Italy. It gouged a 50m hole in her side and she listed, drifted and then rolled onto her starboard side. It took six hours to evacuate the passengers and crew, and thirty-two people died. The story emerged that the captain had taken the wrong route by the island of Giglio for a "sail-by salute". He was tried for manslaughter, causing a maritime accident and abandoning his ship. He was sentenced to sixteen years in jail. When asked about leaving the ship, he apparently said that he "fell into a lifeboat" when the ship rolled over. I well remember the press vilifying him as the story unfolded, calling him "Captain Coward".

Anyone with any connection with physics knew of the Higgs Boson – the so-called "God particle" which scientists had been hoping to discover for a long time. The existence of the particle would confirm the "Standard Model", which was the latest thinking on the structure of matter. At the LHC (Large Hadron Collider) in Cern, a particle with the predicted properties was detected.

UN inspectors found high levels of Uranium enrichment in Iraq. There were concerns that there was no civilian use for such high grade, so there were fears that it was for weapons production. The EU issued an embargo.

2012 was the queen's Diamond Jubilee. (Sixty years on the throne) which had not occurred since Queen Victoria's in 1897, but the celebrations were fairly modest due to the austerity conditions; however, there were celebrations throughout the Commonwealth, culminating in the Jubilee Pageant in London.

The big event for sports fans was, of course, the Olympic Games in London. We were in Cheltenham when the torch bearer, Zara Philips, rode around the racecourse on one leg of the torch relay, but during the games we were back in Spain. The opening ceremony was lauded around the world with praise for the "British sense of humour" for the scene of James Bond accompanying the queen. Glyn had made a mistake with the dates and obtained tickets for events when Nicki, Oliver and Ella would be in Spain with us, so he and Oliver flew back to the UK and straight back again, but they claimed it was worth it. It was a successful game for UK athletes, particularly on super Saturday, when Jessica Ennis-Hill, Greg Rutherford and Mo Farah each won gold within forty-four minutes, in addition to the three golds won earlier in the day. I had always loved watching Jessica Ennis-Hill and was delighted when she was back at the 2016 games, after becoming a mother, to win silver.

I find Spain quite remarkable in its ability to celebrate apparent conflicts. In a town called Crevilliente, not far from San Miguel they hold a "Moors and Christians" parade. In the 8th century, Muslim Umayyad forces from Damascus invaded Spain from the south, via Africa and spread northwards. They built a mosque in Cordoba, second only to the great mosque in Mecca. There were a few Christian communities left in the north, but gradually they grew in strength and in the "Reconquista", begun in the 11th century, succeeded in pushing the Muslims south but were again defeated. For centuries, the battle ebbed and flowed until the Christians finally pushed the Muslims out in the 15th century. Muhammad XII, known as Boabdil, as he fled into exile from Granada, is supposed to have paused at a place now known as "Suspiro del Moro" – the "Moor's sigh" – and viewed the Alhambra one last time. We visited the spot when we were on our way back from Granada. In Crevelliente, the parades go on for two weeks. There is a Captain of the Moors and a King of the Christians. One year, a friend of ours, who is English, but had lived in Crevelliente for twenty years, was elected King of the Christians – a tremendous honour. The next year, he was King of everything! The parades are spectacular with amazing costumes and interesting performers. We were delighted to have a front-row seat – at my height, if I'm one row back, I can't see anything. I have some fantastic photographs.

That year we had the family Christmas in Cheltenham and then were back in Spain, with Steve, for Christmas Day with some neighbours. In Spain, they make more of 12th night – the arrival of the Kings – than they do of Christmas Day. Traditionally, children are given presents on Three Kings Day not Christmas Day, but I suspect canny kids now manage to get both!

In 2013, despite the fate of the Costa Concordia, we decided on a Mediterranean cruise. We had a lovely time, departing from Valencia, visiting Tunis, Carthage, Rome, Marseille and Genoa and returning to Barcelona.

We had several other social highlights that year. Gareth was singing with a choir, and we went on a tour to Alfaz del Pi for a very pleasant weekend. I was dancing with a tap group, and we performed to "All that Jazz". For some time, we had belonged to an organisation called "The U3A" – University of the Third Age. A rather grand name for an organisation aimed at retired people who do not want to vegetate in old age. They held a monthly meeting, social events and there were interest groups on almost every conceivable subject. Gareth and I had been the speakers at one of the meetings; we did a mock TV interview with Gareth as the interviewer, asking predetermined questions, and me as Galileo answering about his life and work. I had suggested a Black-tie ball, and the response was 'Yes, if you organise it', so I did. Prince George, William and Kate's first son was born.

In Egypt, following a military coup; soldiers raided two anti-coup camps. The Muslim brotherhood claimed 2,600 were killed. While Human Rights Watch documented 904 deaths and called it, "one of the world's largest killings of demonstrators in a single day in recent history." The government put the death toll at 624.

The country was shocked and saddened at the murder of off-duty fusilier Lee Rigby in Woolwich by Islamist terrorists. The murderers were British citizens of Nigerian descent who were raised as Christians but later converted to Islam. They claimed they did it to avenge Muslims killed by the British Military. It raised concerns about the radicalisation of young people.

It could be said that a new era began with the Oregon Health and Science University describing the first human embryonic stem cells from cloning. Although there was excitement at the possibilities of major health breakthroughs with the use of stem cells – cells which can be developed into any type of cell – many people were still sceptical of the perils of "playing God" and the possible long-term and, as yet undiscovered, dangers of cloning.

It might seem strange, since we flew a lot, that I should be interested in, rather than intimidated by, TV programmes about plane crashes. I used to watch "Air Crash Investigation". I found it reassuring that when the investigators had arrived at a conclusion, recommendations would be circulated throughout the whole industry, making flying safer. Unlike many situations, where the people say, "lessons will be learned" in the air industry

I think they really are. In 2014, the Malaysian Airways flight 370 crashed mysteriously into the South China Sea, having left Kuala Lumper on a flight to Beijing, with 239 people losing their lives. Communication with air traffic control was lost 38 minutes into the flight. It deviated westward from its flight plan and flew over the Andaman Sea. It crashed when it ran out of fuel. The main part of the fuselage has never been found, but parts which have been identified as coming from Flight 370 washed up on land and were found in 2015 and 2016. Over the years, several searches and investigations were undertaken, but nothing has ever given a satisfactory explanation as to the cause of the crash, despite many theories. It was the deadliest crash for Malaysian airways and the deadliest for a Boeing 777. Following the investigations, procedures were changed to ensure greater reporting while flying over water and new requirements for the ability to recover flight recorders etc. It was the deadliest crash for only a few months, when it was superseded by the downing of Malaysian Airlines scheduled passenger flight seventeen over the Ukraine by a surface-to-air missile by Russian-backed forces, killing all on board. Russia denied any involvement, but I remember seeing convincing evidence on TV that the launch mechanism was transported from Russia into Ukraine beforehand and returned after the attack. Coverage in Russia differed from the rest of the world – the Russians first stated that a Ukrainian Air Force transport plane had been shot down, then claimed that Ukrainian forces had downed the plane. Malaysian Airlines had been struggling for some time, and the two disasters completed its demise. Russia annexed the Crimea and was suspended from G8. Later other sanctions were imposed.

I was appalled again at how terrorists could use children as pawns, with the news of the Chibok schoolgirls kidnapping. An estimated 276 girls and women, mostly Christian, were kidnapped and held hostage by the Islamist terror group Boko Haram in Nigeria. It was ironic that the girls were only in school to take their final physics exam; the school had been closed for four weeks due to the deteriorating situation. Fifty-seven escaped immediately by jumping off the trucks and some have been rescued by various missions and although there are hopes that the rest might be released eventually in exchange for the group's commanders, some are believed to have died. As of 2021, 100 remain missing. Amnesty International estimated in 2015 that at least 2,000 women and girls have been abducted by Boko Haram, many forced into sexual slavery.

Africa was again in the news with the Ebola outbreak. Ebola is a viral infection spread by contact, not by air. The natural carrier is thought to be Fruit bats. 11,310 people died. I remember pictures of a nurse who had been in Africa and diagnosed with Ebola on return to UK. She was in strict isolation amid fears of an epidemic in UK. A vaccine was finally released in 2019.

Steve came over to us and we went to the F1 Grand Prix in Barcelona. It was a good weekend, except for the drifting pollen, which did my hay fever no good at all.

I organised another U3A ball and also a summer party. The party was at a local golf club, with beautiful views over the countryside, and we were treated to a wonderful sunset.

William and Kate's second child, Princess Charlotte was born.

2015 saw al-Qaeda and Boko Haram making the news again – Boko Haram, killing 2,000 in a series of massacres in Nigeria – and two gunmen from al-Qaeda carrying out the notorious attack on the headquarters of the satirical newspaper *Charlie Ebdo* in Paris. The attack sparked an antiterrorism rally attended by over a million people.

Gareth and I were in Vienna for an Oxford alumni weekend, about to leave for the airport to return home, when there was news of an earthquake in Nepal, which triggered avalanches on Everest. It was very traumatic for us because Tim was with an army expedition climbing Everest. Because we were travelling, we had difficulty getting access to computers to get the news, but the first voice report that appeared was actually Tim in a tent with rocks crashing passed him. He was very calm, describing how odd it was that it was not possible to see the danger, as a soldier, he was used to the enemy being in front of him. When Tim had appeared on "This Morning" being interviewed by Eamon Holmes about the expedition, he had suggested that the journalists accompany the expedition, but they said, '*Er*... No... Tell you what, we will give you the kit and you can send back reports,' which is why he was recording his experience. Ironically, Tim's group was following the more difficult route, so they were not in the normal base camp. That camp was more badly hit than Tim's. Twenty-two climbers lost their lives, but in Nepal 8,962 people were killed, nearly 22,000 injured and 3.5 million people were made homeless. Entire villages were destroyed. Long after the TV reports had moved on to other events, Kathmandu continued to struggle to rebuild buildings and lives.

The founding of the first AI research company "Open AI" passed almost unnoticed, considering the all-consuming influence of AI today. I feel that everybody has heard of it, but very few know what it actually is or what the continuing influence will be.

Gwyn and Megan came to us for Christmas, and we visited the beach. When we had first been there on Christmas day, a few years earlier, there had just been a single group of revellers, with picnic table and seats. By now, 2015, there was scarcely space for a single chair anywhere on the beach! We had a lovely Christmas Day meal at a local restaurant, "The Olive Tree".

In some areas of the world, there was an easing of tension: sanctions were lifted against Iran after the IAEA (International Atomic Energy Agency) was satisfied that the nuclear weapons programme had been dismantled, and the US withdrew from Afghanistan after fifteen years.

2016 was a year for family celebrations. In July, it was our 25th wedding anniversary, so we celebrated with a family weekend at the Cotswold Water Park. Steve had been reunited with his long-lost son, Callum, and we were happy to have him with us. The afternoon was spent wakeboarding and a ride on the "spider" – a semi-circular-shaped float towed behind a boat. Ella spectacularly bounced as it went over a wave and unwittingly did a back somersault into the water. Later, we had drinks by the lake, then a lovely meal. The evening became a little boisterous. Tim brought our attention to a challenge to do twenty-two press-ups in as many unusual circumstances as possible. Apparently, twenty-two veterans had committed suicide from PTSD (Post Traumatic Stress Disorder) and the challenge was to increase awareness and acceptance. The intention of Tim's Everest climb had been to shout it from the highest place on Earth that it is OK to admit to stress. Quite a number of press-ups were done that evening! Also, in July, Ollie graduated from Portsmouth University. Glyn and Nicki were with us for their 25th anniversary, in August. In fact, we were quite a crowd. A day at the famous mud treatment at Lo Pagan, further down the coast from San Miguel lead to mud-covered press-ups, and some great photos, though Ella hated it. A visit to the cable-ski in Torrevieja harbour saw Steve complete a jump on his first attempt, but though we had expected even better on subsequent jumps, he didn't succeed in doing it again. Back at our villa, press-ups were completed on the bottom of the pool!

Gareth and I went to Oxford for a St Hilda's reunion dinner – fifty years since I went up. It was lovely to see some of my contemporaries, particularly Janet, who was another of the three of us who went in the same year from Nuneaton High School for Girls, doubling the total number ever to be accepted for Oxford. Steve, Gwyn and Megan were with us for Christmas. We did not know it then, but 2016 was to be the last untroubled year of our lives.

Concerns for the environment were growing steadily as more data were collected. The carbon dioxide level reached 400ppm (parts per million) believed to be the highest in human history. I read a quote recently to the effect that change is inevitable, and the sensible approach is to help wildlife adapt to the speed. I cannot help but agree and though, traditionally, evolution has been seen as a slow process acting over geological timescales, there is some evidence that it can happen in ordinary dimensions. Some recent studies have shown that wildlife *is* managing to adapt.

The UK held a referendum to leave the EU, though the deal would not be finalised until 2020. Prime minister David Cameron had tried to wrest concessions from the EU, and it is my firm belief that if even only small concessions had been forthcoming, the UK would not have left the EU. I do not think the population really understood what effect the departure would have on everyday lives.

2017 in Spain began with snow! We had had hailstorms before, but never snow. It settled just long enough for me to take a picture. Another surprise came one evening as we were having dinner on the balcony. I glanced at the Yuccas and screamed – Gareth nearly choked on his prawns, but it was actually a scream of delight; I could see the beginnings of flower buds. Although they had always grown healthily, the Yuccas had not flowered in eight years – we assumed they would not flower in pots. The next year they flowered again! but never again after that.

In March, Gethin and Sarah came out to celebrate Gethin's 50th birthday. We had a celebration dinner and, as a surprise, I hired Graham Mykall, who performed close-up magic. He was excellent. We had come across a performance of his when we were first in Spain, and when we learned he did house visits, we often hired him to entertain the family, but Gethin and Sarah had never seen him. They were astounded and delighted.

North Korea was again in the news. As far back as 2005, North Korea had stated that they had nuclear weapons, justifying it as protection against the perceived hostility of the US government, though they later agreed to stop their programme in exchange for aid. Despite that, they had carried out tests in 2013 and 2015. This time, they fired a ballistic missile across the Sea of Japan, and again later in the year, they undertook their sixth nuclear test. Kim Jong-nam, the half-brother of the leader Kim Jong-il, was assassinated.

The UN announced the largest humanitarian crisis since World War II as twenty million people in Yemen, Somalia, South Sudan and Nigeria faced famine and starvation. Yemen also had an outbreak of Cholera affecting 200,000 people.

I am sure that many people, like me, were confused by the labels given to various terrorist organisations – al-Qaeda, ISIS, ISIL, and Islamic State. I think I finally grasped that ISIS was the same as ISIL; Islamic State in Iraq and the Levant and both had developed from and/or amalgamated with al-Qaeda. It was ISIS that claimed responsibility for the London Bridge attack, in which a van was deliberately driven into pedestrians on London Bridge, then crashed on Borough High Street, with the three terrorists running into Borough Market and randomly stabbing people. However, it transpired that the bomb outrage at the Ariane Grande concert in Manchester was not the work of ISIS; police believe Salman Abedi acted only with his brother Hashem, sparking concerns again about the radicalisation of young people. Abedi claimed he acted to avenge young Muslims killed in the US-led intervention in the Syrian civil war. In 2014, ISIL seized large parts of Eastern Syria and Western Iraq, causing the US to lead a coalition bombing campaign and provide ground support for the Kurdish-majority Syrian democratic forces. In 2017, ISIL was defeated and Raqqa was liberated.

I was very interested in the reported collision of two neutron stars with detected gravitational and electromagnetic waves. Gravitational waves had been detected two years earlier, but from the collision of two black holes, not neutron stars. The collision also emitted heavy elements such as gold and lead. Although news like this has little impact on the general population, it is of immense interest to the scientific community. Events like this happen only a hundred times in a million years in a galaxy and provide vital evidence to validate or repudiate theories which have made predictions. Laura Cadonati, spokesperson and professor in the school of physics at Georgia Tech said, "The impact for astrophysics is equivalent to the transition from watching a set of still pictures in black and white to sitting in an I-MAX movie theatre. It is a multi-sensory experience of the universe."

Everyone in the UK will remember the Grenfell fire. We

were in London the next morning in a taxi, whose driver described the horror of it all. Seventy died at the scene. It was caused by a fridge fault on the fourth floor. Many investigations have been carried out leading to a variety of conclusions about failings in design, failings in procedures and advice given by fire services and, in particular, to the cladding which had been added to the building in a refurbishment. Although the cladding was deemed to be a cause of the fire spreading so quickly, there are still buildings where the cladding has not been replaced. A sad indictment of human nature is reports of people claiming compensation, falsely claiming to have been in the building or having relatives in there at the time of the fire. Yesterday, I saw a report of another fire in London, in Dagenham. 225 firefighters attended. None were killed, but eighty were evacuated and two taken to the hospital. Although it is yet to be investigated, there appear to be issues similar to Grenfell. The final report on the Grenfell fire came out this week.

We had booked a Warner Leisure Hotel weekend for the family to celebrate my 70th birthday but had to cancel because my 70th birthday present was a diagnosis of breast cancer. The Spanish health service was a little slow to act from my first visit to the doctor, but once they did move, they threw everything at it very rapidly: mammogram, biopsy, MIT scan, and nuclear tracer. The tracer established that it had not spread to the lymph glands. I had a mastectomy on 20th December. I was in and out in a day. We had Christmas dinner at the Olive Tree restaurant, though when I warned the proprietor, June, that we might have to cancel, because I did not know how well I would be, she had generously said she would do a takeaway for us. I was dancing there on New Year's Eve, glad to be alive.

Chapter 26
Post Cancer

In January 2018, I started chemotherapy. I had a friend in the tap dancing group, whom I had watched almost die from cancer. When I had told the group of my diagnosis, she had hugged me and said, 'Be prepared, the treatment is awful, but it is worth it.' In fact, I was not ill at all, apart from a slight cold for the first week and feeling a bit tired. I think it was because her experience of chemotherapy and radiotherapy was for treatment, whereas mine was preventative – they had got all the cancer in the operation. I lost all my hair to the chemo, but took to wearing a turban for daytime, and a blonde wig for evenings. It made a change to be blonde. I looked at pretty turbans online and found them very expensive, but I came across a series of plain one-colour ones at a reasonable price, which had a belt carriage to take a scarf or band. I decided the answer was to buy about three turbans, say, black, beige and blue and get pretty scarfs to alternate. I had been doing silk paining so I started to make hand-dyed silk scarves. I was pleased with the results and later used to make and sell them at craft fayres.

Warner's had been very good. I had not taken cancellation insurance, but when I rang up, the customer service rep said that under the circumstances, they would treat the insurance as retrospective, so that all I had to pay was the £40 insurance premium and was given a credit for a future booking. There was a brief window between chemo and radiotherapy, so we rearranged the Warner Leisure weekend. The Hotel had a no children policy, to which we were attracted, wanting a grown-up experience, but we had not realised that their definition of children was under twenty-five. The grandchildren and boyfriends/girlfriends were all about twenty-one, so we started to coach them in what was their date of birth if challenged, but in the end, we went to a restaurant just down the road for lunch, then they headed to Portsmouth for a reunion party. Gareth, Glyn, Nicki, Steve and I had a lovely meal.

The radiotherapy was intrusive because it was a thirty-minute journey; it was every day for six weeks, and there was a lot of waiting about, but I did not burn or have any other adverse effects. It also meant we could not plan a holiday anywhere that year, but we did have another lovely family celebration in Cardiff in December for Gareth's 80th birthday.

Outside of our personal concerns, we did have a chance to notice a few events. 2018 was the year the Windrush Scandal broke. The problem originated in 1948, when many people from British Colonies such as the Caribbean, were encouraged to come to Britain to fill the gap left by World War II labour shortages. Many came on "HMT Empire Windrush". They were not given documentation. The law changed in 1973, but in 2018, a more hostile environment to illegal immigration saw many people unable to prove that they had been here legally before 1973. They were threatened with deportation, denied legal rights and detained. Despite a compensation scheme being announced in December 2018, by 2021 hardly any people had been compensated and some died before having any redress.

Russia was in the news for two completely different reasons. They were denied entry to the Olympic Games, being accused of State sponsored doping, though a few athletes who could show that they were not involved were allowed to compete under a different flag. The other event was more serious. Former military officer and double agent Sergei Skripal and his daughter Yulia were poisoned with Novichok, a nerve agent, in an assassination attempt. Russia denied any involvement, but British authorities identified two Russian nationals using false names. Twenty-eight countries supported Britain, but still Russia denied everything and even accused British authorities of carrying out the poisoning. Russian diplomats were expelled, but again, Russia denied everything and retaliated by expelling foreign diplomats. A policeman who had investigated the Skripal's house was also hospitalised and later two other people, at a site quite close to Salisbury, suffered effects. It is thought that that was the result of careless disposal of a perfume bottle containing some Novichok, by the two Russians. I remember being astounded by a TV report, in which it was said that the Russians had claimed they were "merely tourists" and had travelled to London, then to Salisbury to see the "World-famous cathedral tower", which at 123 m is the tallest in Britain. It sounded about as believable as snow on the Equator! The episode bore echoes of Litvenenko, assassinated by poisoning with polonium-210 in 2006. Again, Russia had denied any involvement, but the European Court of Human Rights ruled against them.

    We had breathed a sigh of relief at surviving and were looking forward to better times, but it was not to be. In 2019, Glyn, Gareth's eldest son, was on a charity cycle ride in Wales; when he dropped from the bike. Marshalls performed CPR, and he was airlifted to Morriston Hospital, but he was in a coma. We flew over from Spain as soon as we could. It was all such a shock and seemed so unfair. He was fifty-five and very fit; he did marathons and triathlons. He and Nicki were so happy, with Ollie and Ella on the cusp of being grown up and independent. Every time the doctors tried to bring him out of the coma, he started to fit. It transpired he had had a blocked artery, so the CPR had been ineffective, and he had been without oxygen for about half an hour. We were offered end-of-life counselling and Glyn was allowed to go peacefully, with other patients benefitting from his organs.

Despite The New York Times declaring 2019 to be the "best year in human history", there were still concerns. Particularly about climate change. July was reported as the hottest on record, and there were extreme weather events such as fires in the Canary Island and the Amazon rain forest and floods in India. Hurricane Dorian, which hit the Bahamas, was the strongest ever recorded. 500,000 people marched in Canada, and 4,000,000 worldwide went on strike.

There were problems in Hong Kong with 1,000,000 people protesting over extradition terms to China, the largest protest since the 1987 handover of Hong Kong to China from the UK at the expiry of the lease. The protests continued throughout 2019 and beyond. There was also tension between traditional foes: The US left the Intermediate-Range Nuclear Forces Treaty, citing Russian non-compliance. Russia responded by withdrawing also. Iran was found to have breached the permitted levels of Uranium enrichment and shot down a US drone, so the US sent 1000 extra troops. The US also accused the Chinese firm Hauwei of fraud and sparked a tit-for-tat trade war with China.

At the end of 2019, the report of a death from a new virus in Wuhan, China went almost unnoticed, but that soon changed. In January 2020 China confirmed an outbreak of a human-to-human transferrable virus, initially called SARS (Severe Acute Respiratory Syndrome) later commonly known as COVID-19. It was not known then, but it would eventually cause over 7,000,000 deaths worldwide (some sources put it at over

15,000,000) and cause the largest worldwide recession since the 1930s. I remember the first time I heard of it was a report of passengers on a cruise ship in Japan being quarantined. The Diamond Princess was on a cruise from Yokohama and was returning after stopping in Hong Kong. The captain received a report from officials that a passenger who had disembarked had since tested positive for Covid-19. In the first round of testing, 10 cases were reported, but that rapidly escalated. The crew were woefully unprepared for such an emergency, as no one really knew how to tackle the problem. Of the 3700 on board, 712 cases were detected, and fourteen people are said to have died, though it is difficult to state the exact cause of death for some of the elderly passengers.

By the beginning of March, we were reading reports in the UK press, but it still did not seem to impact us in Spain. For quite a time, there were no cases in San Miguel. We were stunned when, one Friday morning in the local shop, there was talk that all the bars and restaurants in Spain would be closed from Saturday night. It was announced initially for a fortnight. With hindsight, I am glad that we were not told how long it would be – the prospect would have been very daunting. I found it surreal, as if an unseen monster was lurking just behind you, but just might be a figment of your imagination. Lockdown meant no one was allowed to go out except to the doctor's, hospital or supermarket, and the supermarket had to be the closest one to you. A later addition to the rules was only one person was allowed in a car; then prescribed exercise periods for nominated groups of people. At first, it was not known whether the disease was contagious (spread by contact) or infectious (droplet infection through the air), hence the raft of measures such as hand sanitizing, minimum distance, fist bumping instead of shaking hands face masks, etc. Later, it was established that the main vector was droplet infection, so face masks and distancing lasted longer than some of the other restrictions. Bars and restaurants were finally allowed to reopen in May, still with certain restrictions. I have a lovely photo of Gareth and me at a favourite restaurant; our first trip out since the pandemic began. Little did I know that five weeks later, he would be dead.

 Gareth awoke in the early hours of the morning one Friday in June with a terrible headache and asked me to get him some paracetamol. He said he did not want me to call a doctor, but when he was no better, I called an ambulance. By the time the ambulance arrived, Gareth was unconscious, and when we got to the hospital, although they did tests, and the doctor spoke to me carefully, he was really saying there was no way back – the brain haemorrhage was unstoppable. I was devastated. Oliver, Gethin and Agnelle were with me by Saturday night – they must have got the first allowed flight out to Spain. Gethin, Oliver and Agnelle stayed until Tuesday and Steve arrived as they left. Gareth had not recovered consciousness. We both had funeral plans in place, but Gareth wanted to be buried in Wales, so there was still a lot of arranging to do. Steve and I managed to get flights back for 15th July, and the funeral was arranged for the 24th in Brecon. There were still restrictions in place, so only a few people were allowed to attend the graveside ceremony. There were beautiful views across the valley, but this being Wales, it rained heavily. The ceremony began with Gareth's favourite song "Dock of the Bay" by Otis Redding and included the Welsh hymn "Gwhoddiad", which had been played at his father's funeral and at Glyn's. We ended listening to "Concierto de Aranjuez" by Spain's only well-known composer, Rodrigo, and a favourite of ours. As the strains of the guitar and harp floated across the valley, the clouds parted, and a ray of sunshine pierced the gloom. I'm sure everyone was as moved as I was.

Chapter 27
Life After Gareth

They say that you should not make any major decisions for at least six months after a bereavement, but Steve and I did not have that luxury. I had to consider my options. I knew that life would never be the same without Gareth, but I did not think that going back to the UK would be the answer. Steve had reconnected with an old Australian friend who had visited him in Cheltenham, but she had returned to Australia to sort out a visa. Leanne did not like the weather in the UK, so we talked about the three of us setting up a glamping business in Spain. If we decided to do it, it must be before December 2020, since that was when the Brexit conditions would finally take effect, and after that, Steve would find it impossible to get a residencia in Spain. Leanne got caught up in the COVID restrictions and had to stay in Australia until January 2021. By the end of August, Steve and I had completed all the necessary paperwork, though it did seem that every organisation just made everything as difficult as possible, at a time when all you want to do is grieve. We made the decision to sell the house and go to Spain.

There were still some restrictions in place, but Steve cheered me up by devising allowable picnics and excursions. We bought a one-bedroomed flat and Steve renovated it. It came in useful when Callum came out to see us, since it was not yet rented out. I had a lovely surprise when Callum made me a birthday cake. He went back before Christmas, but Steve and I spent it in the flat, since it was within walking distance of one of our favourite restaurants, where we had Christmas lunch.

In the New Year, the flat was rented out and Leanne was finally released to join us. There was still a restriction that you could not travel outside your own province, so we were not able to start looking for suitable land or properties; we had to content ourselves with internet research. Finally, we were allowed to travel and since we had decided that the location for our project should be Andalucia, with its easy access to the coast, the mountains and cities such as Granada, Seville and Cordoba, whilst also being in easy reach of Malaga airport. We rented a property in Velas, Malaga, for a month, so that we could look around the region. We found a piece of land, 110,000 sqm with two houses on it, much in need of repair, just outside a typical Andalucian whitewashed village called Casarabonela. It was on the top of a hill and had wonderful 360-degree views. Unfortunately, the last 5km of the approach road were steep and difficult, not too off-putting for most people, but for me. I knew I would not be able to drive up it or cycle or walk, so we changed the plan and decided I would move relatively close by to a residential caravan park, while Steve and Leanne would take on the project. Surprisingly, we were able to coordinate the sale of the house in Cheltenham and the villa in San Miguel and move at the end of May. Steve and Leanne stayed in my new home for a while, with Steve driving up to work on Casarabonela each day. Sadly, Steve and Leanne's relationship faltered, and Leanne returned to Australia leaving Steve somewhat marooned in his eerie.

I had received my first Covid vaccine at the end of 2020 in San Miguel and returned to receive the second one in June. By then three billion vaccines had been administered worldwide, but in India the death toll was 250,000 with reports of bodies washed up on the banks of the Ganges. The whole world was impacted by the Covid pandemic and understandably people felt their lives had been devasted by it, but to put it in perspective, the total death toll is estimated at about five million, whereas the death toll in the 1918 flu epidemic, at its lowest estimate was 17.4 million, with some estimates much, much higher.

Despite the fact that the Treaty on the Prohibition of Nuclear Weapons came into effect, and the US had finally withdrawn from Afghanistan, there were still tensions and flash points; North Korea demonstrated ballistic missiles to land just outside Japanese waters, and almost immediately South Korea demonstrated its first submarine-launched ballistic missile.

One ominous portent was a buildup of Russian forces on Ukraine's borders, with Russia warning NATO against sending troops.

In 2022, despite the five permanent members of the UN Security Council: China, France, Russia, US and UK issuing a joint statement to the effect that a nuclear could not be won and must never be fought, which looked promising for the future peace of the world, within two months Russia invaded Ukraine – the largest armed conflict in Europe since WWII. I remember thinking, "I can't see an end to this", because Ukraine was scarcely strong enough to withstand the attacks and Putin seemed unlikely to listen to anyone else's reasoning. Though other countries took various measures and applied sanctions, no one wanted to risk starting a world war, so countries did not get directly involved. Problems with fuel and other supplies compounded the effects of the Covid pandemic to have impact on the economic health of many nations.

More encouraging for the future of the world was the news

that the most promising progress in fusion power since 1997 had been achieved at the JET (Joint European Taurus) project in Oxford, with double the previous power output and also that the LHC (Large Hadron Collider) had been recommissioned following an upgrade.

It was Queen Elizabeth II's Platinum Jubilee (70 years on the throne), but unfortunately, she was not to see the end of the year, dying in September. An outpouring of national grief paid tribute to her dedication and life of service to the Nation. Charles succeeded her as King, with Camilla as Queen.

That year would be my 75th birthday, but again, like the queen, I had an official birthday, because I wanted Nicki, Ollie and Ella to be able to be with me, and both Nicki and Ella were constrained to school holidays, so I held the celebration in October during the half-term holiday. We had a wonderful disco in the Parque event room.

Steve had had a hard time in Casarabonela, but towards the end of the year he met Natasja, a lovely Dutch lady. Steve and I had a celebration dinner just before Christmas, at a beautiful Hotel, with extensive grounds, Cortijo Sabila, in Villa Nueva del Rosario just outside Antequera.

Steve proposed to Natasja and they set the wedding for May. I investigated the procedure for a marriage in Spain, but it appeared so complicated that a better route seemed to be to get married in Gibraltar (under British law) and then have the celebration in Spain. The date for the ceremony in Gibraltar was May 12th and the celebration was the day after in the Cortijo Sabila. I grew anxious in April as the weather was glorious and I thought, *It can't go on like this all the way to September – it must break at some point – just don't let it be May 13th*. Nicki, Ollie, Megan and Gwyn were able to be with us, with Ollie as best man, along with a few other of Steve's old friends and Tash's family. In the morning Nicki and I sat on my decking looking up at the cloudy sky with the hotel phoning to ask if we wanted to move the celebration inside. We decided to risk it outside, and fortunately, the clouds cleared, and it was a lovely afternoon. In fact, if it had been any warmer, the buffet would have dried up before we could eat it. We were able to swim in the pool and play chess on the huge outdoor chessboard, before the evening disco. I had taught Tash's daughter and two of her friends a belly dance routine, so Tash, I and the girls performed, much to the delight of the guests. Steve and Tash honeymooned in Thailand.

Our own preparations rather distracted us from the Coronation of King Charles III and Queen Camilla. I remember seeing a TV documentary about the Coronation of Queen Elizabeth, seventy years earlier – I had never seen it before, because we had not had a TV at that time. I was interested to see how different this coronation would be. I realised how steeped in history and tradition, and how dictated by religion, in particular, the Christian religion, it had been. It would obviously not be so appropriate in a multicultural society such as we have today.

In the wider world, there was an increasing frequency of extreme events: earthquakes in Turkey, Syria, Morocco and Afghanistan, leaving over 66,000 dead; cyclones in Malawi, Mozambique and Libya, killing over 11,000; tornadoes in the USA.

Although the news reports had largely moved on, there was still conflict between Israel and Palestine. Brief periods of respite do not alter the underlying problems. I fear there is no resolution to the fact that Palestinians see the land as theirs and Israelis see it as theirs. We were also hearing less about Ukraine, but that did not mean that Russian aggression had abated.

AI was actually founded as an academic discipline in 1956, but it is really only relatively recently that strides in application have been made. I was bought a book on the future of science way back in about 2012 and found the content rather far-fetched, particularly the AI, but of course, it is now becoming commonplace. Despite my science background, I must admit to some trepidation about the use of AI, and its role in our lives. I think it might turn out to be a double-edged sword.

2024 was an Olympic year. I saw a programme about the 1948 Olympics, which Britain rescued: by agreeing to host the games. I was surprised that I had never heard anything about it. Just after the end of the war, not everyone was convinced that hosting the Olympics in the bombed-out city of London was a good decision. But businessmen and volunteers rallied round to make the event a great success. Of course, it was all amateur then. The programme showed Dorothy Tyler, who won a silver medal in the high jump, practising by jumping over the washing line in her garden! It had only been in 1900 that women were allowed to compete, and indeed,, there were many events which were not open to women. I remember clearly that when I was at school, the longest distance for women to run was 800yds. This year, 2024, is the first in which there is gender parity, and Sifan Hassan of the Netherlands emphasised their suitability to compete by winning bronze in the 5,000m, 10,000m and gold in the marathon. I was also struck by the changes in the Opening Ceremony over the years. It used to be stadium-centred with emphasis on the athletes and the paying audience, but it seems to me that now the emphasis is on a worldwide TV audience and what appeals to that mass audience, not so much about the games – advertising and sponsorship to the fore. I feel sorry for the paying audience in the stadium who just see it on large TV screens.

Watching the Paralympics, I was reminded of the origins. Although sport for impaired athletes has existed for over 100 years, it was not until the Stoke Mandeville hospital was set up after WWII, to rehabilitate veterans, that it really became mainstream. Sport was used first to motivate and rehabilitate, then for recreation and finally for competitive purposes.

Early in 2024, Britain was saddened by the announcement that both King Charles and Catherine, Princess of Wales had cancer. Catherine was determined to make her reappearance at public events, the Trooping of the Colour for the King's official birthday in June, but looked rather thin and pale. Charles continued to carry out our royal duties but sometimes looked a little weary and drawn.

I was appalled at the scandal of the sub-postmasters; not just that it should happen in the first place, but that it took many years and a film for those concerned to begin to be taken seriously. I cannot imagine how it must have felt to know that you were innocent and hit a brick wall in trying to be heard – even to the extent of being put in jail. I think it illustrates again the dangers of utter reliance and confidence in technology. This did not just happen – there were people responsible for the suffering, who should have taken action.

The world is still in an unstable state. There is continuing tension between the US and Iraq and Syria following a deadly drone attack on a US military base, and Russia is still attempting to invade Ukraine. The situation in Israel and Gaza shows no sign of improvement.

I think everyone was as shocked as I was at the murder of three young girls at a dance class in Southport. Perhaps almost as upsetting was the aftermath, in which erroneous social media reports circulated, pointing the finger at an asylum seeker and Muslims, causing revenge attacks on a mosque.

By this time, we had realised that we were underfunded for the project at Casarabonela. Tash had been living on a rented property, which, although it had land, had a house in a fairly poor state of repair. She and Steve began living in the house, with Steve attempting to carry out improvements. The opportunity came up to buy the property, so we decided that the best course of action would be to sell Casarabonela and my home, buy Tash's place, and I move into a van at the bottom of the garden. My van sold very quickly, and Casaredia have been to make sure that the site is suitable to put the van, so a new chapter opens…

Conclusion

There is so much more I could have included. Every day, something jogs another memory. The most difficult decisions were what to leave out and the relative balance between personal, national and worldwide events. I have noticed, as I read it, though, that in the early years the emphasis is on the personal, whereas later it shifts towards national and worldwide. This may be a consequence of the self-centred viewpoint of a young person, or the lack of information available then compared to today, or a combination of both. There are a number of themes which I think characterise the time period.

The attitude to the position of women and their available options has clearly changed dramatically, perhaps stimulated by women taking over traditional male roles during WWII. Also, attitudes to homosexuality and gender differentiation have undergone a sea change, going from being illegal to being protected rights.

Agreements made after WWII might have been the root cause of some of today's continuing conflicts: the partition of India and Pakistan; Israel and Palestine; and Russia and Ukraine. Global distrust and desire for power and influence in regions of the world also account for many of the tensions and flare-ups e.g. USA, Iraq, Iran, China and Japan. The spectre of nuclear war hung over much of the time from 1947.

Increasing knowledge has spawned changes in attitude: laws on drink-driving; restrictions on smoking; concern for the effects of global warming and climate change, sustainable farming, pollution of the oceans by plastics.

I happened to see a few screenings of a game show from the '60s to more recent the other day and it struck me that many of the changes in society can be seen in the shows; not just fashions and hairstyles, but the job titles, demeanour of the contestants, what were considered as sought-after prizes, and perhaps most tellingly the role of the female contestants, mainly "housewife, secretary or hairdresser".

Perhaps most people would consider the influence of technology to be the biggest change. Certainly, there is a world of difference from the "Brownie" camera which I used as a teenager, which used film which had to be loaded then removed when full and sent away to be developed, to today's digital cameras. Many people no longer print out photos, just share them, then store them on devices. Indeed, there is little need for the camera at all, since phones have such good camera facility. The mobile phone has changed the way people behave, giving them the freedom to change arrangements at short notice and spend hours "chatting" and playing on their mobiles. I have just seen a report of concerns about young people not spending enough time outdoors connecting with nature, and we have almost gone from worrying about suntan factors to protect from sun damage to worrying about lack of vitamin D – the sunshine vitamin, which can only be manufactured by the body in the presence of sunlight, and is not readily available in foods. The internet has given people a vast source of information, but also given opportunity for misinformation and changing who has influence - not necessarily for the better. "Bloggers" regale their followers with chat. Extremists have the opportunity for their views to reach a large audience. Streaming services for music and film have altered the landscape for those industries. Newspapers, the BBC and ITV are no longer the main source of news, altering who has control over the content. The scene has changed for marketing, giving rise to more freedom of expression and leading to emphasis on presentation and special effects rather than product information. Images which would have been unthinkable in the '50s now regularly appear on our screens. So-called "Reality" TV shows are anything but real; depicting behaviour that would have been unthinkable a generation ago. So-called cyber-crimes have proliferated: identity theft, scans and cons of increasing sophistication.

Covid was an event which not only affected the financial situation of the whole world, but also gave rise to permanent changes in working practices and attitudes.

I used to watch the programme "Tomorrow's World" but a recent retrospective showed how few of the predictions or devices discussed on the programme actually came to fruition. Who can say where tomorrow will take us? I think the biggest impact will be use of AI and I still maintain that mankind MUST conquer the use of nuclear fusion for power generation.